CREATION
HOUSE

EVERYTHING

You Ever Wanted to Know About

SEX and GENDER

AND THE BIBLE

WHAT'S HOT, AND WHAT'S NOT ACCORDING TO SCRIPTURE

NANCY ESKIJIAN

Everything You Ever Wanted to Know About Sex and
Gender and the Bible: What's Hot, and What's Not
According to Scripture
By Nancy Eskijian
Published by Creation House
A Charisma Media Company
600 Rinehart Road
Lake Mary, Florida 32746
www.charismamedia.com

Unless otherwise noted, all Scripture quotations are from the King James Version of the Bible.

Design Director: Bill Johnson
Cover design by Nancy Panaccione

Visit the author's website: www.labreadoflife.org

Library of Congress Cataloging-in-Publication Data: 2012933340
International Standard Book Number: 978-1-61638-954-3
E-book International Standard Book Number: 978-1-61638-955-0

13 14 15 16 17 — 9 8 7 6 5 4 3
Printed in the United States of America

DEDICATION

To Jesus Christ

The Bridegroom of the Church

TABLE OF CONTENTS

INTRODUCTION

The Foundations

I HAVE BEEN A pastor for many years and an observer of the trends in society. This book is mainly for believers, because the church of Jesus Christ must return to its first love, Jesus Christ, from whom all other loves flow. By this we gain a foundational understanding of His character, who He wants us to be and become, and how we are to relate to each other and the world. He is the author of love and life, and we are to be a city set on a hill, and the light of the world.

I initially wrote the outline of this book just to help the congregation I serve. It started out as a Bible study, among others placed on our "literature rack" at the church. There seemed to be a combination of confusion, ignorance, and disobedience in this area, which led to disasters and grief; and, importantly, lives out of God's will, order, and blessing. We ministered to many people who experienced the emotional, spiritual, and physical fallout of their (or someone else's) choices. I wanted God's people to understand His ways, His heart, His purposes, and His Word. God's view of marriage, sexuality, and gender are basic issues that the church needs to embrace. These are revival issues. Honestly, I did not want to write this book, but once started, I knew it was a manifesto of faith that had to be finished, for the time being anyway.

The Scriptures state in Psalm 11:3, "If the foundations be destroyed, what can the righteous do?" The psalmist poses a good question for today. What can the righteous do? And are we righteous? The answer is simple: We are the righteous if we believe the truth, yield to the truth, live the truth, be the truth, and speak the truth in love. Jesus came to be a witness to the truth (John 18:37). So are we.

The Word of God is foundational, and marriage is foundational in the Word of God. Identity in Christ as He defines it is foundational. Sexual expression in marriage is foundational. And God's power and grace to change hearts and behavior are foundational. He is either God or He is not. He is either the origin of life or not. He is either the "Resurrection and the Life" or He is not. If He is who He says He is, then His Word and ways are to be respected and obeyed. God and His Word are one. Remember our faith is about the God of the Cross and the Resurrection, through which we experience the expanse of God's love in saving us. First we die to our ways, and then we live. It is His pattern and it is His sole offer and only way to obtain abundant, eternal, supernatural, and resurrection life. But there is a cost—the old life dies, so the new life can emerge.

Everything You Ever Wanted to Know... is a teaching on the divine foundation of human life on this planet, and a teaching to reveal the heart of our Creator and Savior, in our daily lives, in our intimate longings, and our fruitfulness for the kingdom and eternity. It also simply teaches what the Bible has to say about the subject. Sexual expression, gender, and all human relationships have a spiritual dimension that reflects God's order, plan, design, and desires. We must ask who we are as the people of God. This really is not about "dos and don'ts"—though there are guidelines, blessings, and consequences described in Scripture—but living out His life in us. I like Eugene Peterson's version of the Bible, *The Message*. Romans 12:1 states: "So here's what I want you to do, God helping you: Take your everyday, ordinary life—your sleeping, eating, going-to-work, and walking-around life—and place it before God as an offering. Embracing what God does for you is the best thing you can do for him." Yes, it is our everyday, ordinary, sleeping, eating, going-to-work, walking-around life that is an offering to God, and through that ordinary, flesh and blood life we live out His life and glorify Him in this world.

What you read in this book may seem impossible, irrelevant, or even foolish to you, but remember Jesus said that straight is the gate and narrow is the way that leads to life, and few there be that find it (Matt. 7:14). Notice the way leads to "life," but few actually find it. The Lord is merciful, gracious, longsuffering, and abundant in goodness and truth; and if we follow His ways, they lead to life. The Word guides us and the Holy Spirit enables and empowers His life in us. He is the great Lover, Lord, Law, and Life of the universe. If we allow the Lord to do His work of love and truth in our hearts—embracing what He does for us—we will not only find Him, but ourselves, and be able to relate to others in right relationship. In the process we reclaim the power, peace, authority, and destiny that He has desired for us from the foundation of the world.

You should know that this book is about what God says. It's "BC"—Biblically Correct. I didn't make it up. It is not "politically correct," for it expresses a covenant view of sexuality and sexual expression, and the Creator's view of life itself. This book is for those who want to understand the biblical view of sex, gender, holiness, and wholeness. This is a spiritual book meant to be downloaded and burned into our hearts by the fire of the Holy Spirit.

> Those from among you shall build the old waste places; You shall raise up the foundations of many generations; And you shall be called the Repairer of the Breach, The Restorer of Streets to Dwell In.
>
> —Isaiah 58:12, nkjv

Part I

MARRIAGE AND SEX

God's Divine Plan

*All the paths of the LORD are mercy and truth unto
such as keep his covenant and his testimonies.*
—PSALM 25:10

Sex is a very holy subject.
—GEDDES MACGREGOR[1]

*He restores my soul; He leads me in the paths
of righteousness for His name's sake.*
—PSALM 23:3, NKJV

PRINCIPLE NUMBER ONE: FOLLOW THE PATTERN

*Thy kingdom come, Thy will be done
in earth, as it is in heaven.*
—MATTHEW 6:10

THIS IS THE beginning of a great divine love story—how God wanted to give pleasure to man and woman, and design a race of people who would be created in His image and likeness. To accomplish this, He provided gender, sexuality, marriage, and sexual expression. The Lord intended human life to be holy, not in some strange or unattainable way, but to have a divine dimension, connected to Him and like Him. So it is only natural and supernatural that the very relations that create and sustain life should be aligned with the holy and divine order described in Scripture. We are God's love children, created in His image and bought with the blood of Jesus. Creation and salvation are two extravagant sides of the divine quest for love.

Let's look at the big plan: People created in His image.

Marriage and Sex: God Invented It! God Approves of It! God Delights in It!

Because of its great power, pleasure, purpose, passion, and potential, God established sexual expression to be protected in the boundaries of marriage. For what purposes? For purposes of *pleasure, bonding, intimacy, unity, procreation* (having children), *companionship*, and many other reasons.

God is in favor of life. He is the Multiplier and the Giver of joy, and so He designed people in His image and likeness to keep life and love going and growing. He added pleasure to the act of sexual relations so that people would want to engage in it, bond with and love each other, and "be fruitful and multiply, fill the earth and subdue it" (Gen. 1:28, NKJV), among other reasons. God created pleasure, folks, think about it. Our flesh and desires is not some strange realm He doesn't know about. He put it all together—body, soul, and spirit. With marriage a man and woman become one creation, according to Scripture. That means something totally new is created in the world—one person is created out of two, and the two become one, a unit expressing itself in two persons. Add Jesus to the family, and you have three in one. Come to think about it, that is a little like the Godhead, three in *one*—a unit expressing itself in three Persons!

Marriage Is God's Idea, Not Man's

The idea of marriage goes back to the Garden of Eden, when the woman was taken out of the side of the man. God invented marriage upon the creation of woman.

And the Lord God caused a deep sleep to fall upon Adam, and he slept; and he took one of his ribs, and closed up the flesh instead thereof; And the rib, which the Lord God had taken from man, made he a woman, and brought her unto the man. And Adam said, This is now bone of my bones, and flesh of my flesh: she shall be called Woman, because she was taken out of Man Therefore shall a man leave his father and his mother, and shall cleave unto his wife: and they shall be one flesh.

—Genesis 2:21–24

Marriage is the first human covenantal relationship. It has spiritual, emotional, mental, physical, sexual, financial, governmental, and societal significance.

The definition of gender originated even earlier, and is directly related to the divine nature itself—which is a very profound concept.

Then God said, "Let Us make man in Our image, according to Our likeness; let them have dominion over the fish of the sea, over the birds of the air, and over the cattle, over all the earth and over every creeping thing that creeps on the earth." So God created man in His own image; in the image of God He created him; male and female He created them. Then God blessed them, and God said to them, "Be fruitful and multiply; fill the earth and subdue it; have dominion over the fish of the sea, over the birds of the air, and over every living thing that moves on the earth."

—Genesis 1:26–28, nkjv

The attributes of God are seen in the very creation of man and woman: Dominion, unity, fruitfulness—three of the most powerful attributes of the Godhead; male and female, created

He them and He blessed them. God's personhood includes male and female attributes.

The Scripture gives some further insight on the creation of woman:

> And the Lord God said, "It is not good that man should be alone; I will make him a helper comparable to him."
>
> —Genesis 2:18, nkjv

Many teachers have provided revelation on this—I think it is enough to say that man and woman together is a divine combination. The woman as "helper" is not a servant or personal assistant to the man in Scripture. Interestingly, the word is the same as the word "Helper" used for the Holy Spirit in the Book of John. I believe the woman was intended to bring more of God to the man. Woman brings completion for a divine purpose. Jesus died for men and women, male and female—so both are part of His divine plan, both are bought with the blood of Jesus, and both are equally valuable.

There is a direct relationship to the divine nature and gender. He made male and female in His image and likeness. Gender has become a battleground issue today, and so has marriage. Marriage is a covenantal relationship established by God, and, as we will see, it is an earthly representation of the covenantal relationship between Christ and His church—on earth as it is in heaven. Gender, marriage, and sexuality are interrelated foundational creations on earth, and interrelated foundational patterns from God in heaven, in order to release His purposes on earth and give joy to His creation. Therefore, they are not to be taken lightly or out of context with regard to the divine plan. While many people don't believe this, or care about this, and would never accept this as true, spinning gender and sexual expression into many directions, the purpose here is to provide a foundational understanding for the people of God in the context of the divine pattern.

Jesus restated the Genesis scripture in Mark 10:6–9 (NLT):

> But God's plan was seen from the beginning of
> creation, for "He made them male and female. This
> explains why a man leaves his father and mother
> and is joined to his wife, and the two are united into
> one." Since they are no longer two but one, let no one
> separate them, for God has joined them together.

Notice what Jesus says about marriage and gender in the above scripture—it is God's plan. Let's follow the pattern—if we follow the pattern we cannot get lost.

From the beginning of creation, God created male and female, and He physically designed them to be joined together. First, God identifies human gender as male and female. (Note: God didn't create a third sex or fourth sex.) Male and female, and their unity together, are God's *creative order*, and again, relate to the image of God. Claiming a different identity based on disposition or desire does not mean a new gender has been created or alternate gender attained. I think it is important to determine what we mean here. Follow the pattern of God's creative order.

The married couple becomes one flesh and they need to leave family or origin behind to start something new. The Lord sets out a *personal governmental order*, the family unit, with husband and wife, mother and father (if there are children). The man departs from one home to create another governmental structure with himself and his wife. And so creation multiplies and grows within a committed unit.

As the man cleaves to his wife, they become one flesh. Neither is to be self-identified any more, but identified in the new family unit. This is an important spiritual concept too; as we enter into Christ, we are no longer just self-identified, but part of Him. A new creation has occurred in the merging of man and woman—they become one flesh. Marriage reflects the divine purpose of God, through our relationship with Him, to form a new creation through *covenantal order*. When we come to the Lord we merge with His body spiritually through the Holy Spirit and become a new creation—His body and bride—under the new covenant.

The family unit is where the Lord sets out human *sexual order*, because it is the God-ordained relationship for sexual relations uniting the God-designed creations for sexual relations (not male and male, or female and female). This order is between man and woman. Sexual expression is to occur in the boundaries of marriage, as the Scripture clearly shows in Mark 10:5–9.

Reproductive order: A new creation has occurred (man and woman as one) to give birth in the natural to other new creations (babies), just as Christ is married to His church (a new creation), and that union expands His family (spiritual babies).

God's stamp of approval is on marriage because it reflects a *divine pattern of Christ and His church*. So, the union reflects a *divine order*. Marriage is something God joins together—that is the Christian ideal—I'm not talking about the world's view; therefore, be led of God in marriage choices. It is ordained of God, and a design that God approves and originates. That is why it is called "holy matrimony." We have moved from creative order to divine order in marriage.

In fact all of creation and redemption (God's act of love to give us a new life through the death and resurrection of Jesus Christ) is reflected in the marriage relationship and covenant. Creation and re-creation: Old lives being left for new lives in the marriage. The New Testament instructs a husband to love his wife as Christ loved the church and gave Himself for her. Therefore, the pattern and significance of marriage is foundational and profound. It has roots in heaven and on earth, just as other profound realities in the Bible such as the sacrificial blood, the ark of the covenant, and the very tabernacle of God. The mystery of marriage is the mystery of Christ and His church:

For this cause shall a man leave his father and mother,
and shall be joined unto his wife, and they two shall
be one flesh. This is a great mystery: but I speak
concerning Christ and the church.

—EPHESIANS 5:31–32

THE LORD INTENDS THAT THE COUPLE EXPRESS THEMSELVES SEXUALLY IN THE RELATIONSHIP AND BOUNDARIES OF MARRIAGE

The Word of God shows us that marriage and sexual relations in marriage are a holy combination. Scripture makes this clear in direct reference to the "marriage bed," and provides express warnings about sex outside of the marriage relationship.

Hebrews 13:4 (NLT) says, "Give honor to marriage, and remain faithful to one another in marriage. God will surely judge people who are immoral and those who commit adultery." Another translation: Marriage in every way must be held in honor, and the marriage bed unpolluted, but fornicators and adulterers God will judge (those who sin sexually whether single or married.) The King James Version says: "Marriage is honorable in all, and the bed undefiled."

What does this scripture say? Marriage is honorable, and honor comes with marriage for all people, even people who don't know God, who married for the wrong reasons, who have a multitude of problems, or couldn't care less. It is not a shameful relationship in and of itself, it is honorable. There is a respect, dignity, and covering that comes with marriage that does not come with fornication.

What about the marriage bed? The "marriage bed" is unpolluted, or it is spiritually clean, because it is in God's plan and order. There is no shame to the marriage bed. God is in favor of sexual relations in marriage, and only in marriage. We can go further to say that the marriage bed itself should not be polluted. Just because two people are married does not mean the "marriage bed" is to be sexually degrading.

The immoral—those who engage in fornication and adultery, or illicit (unlawful, in that it is not recognized by God, or, in some cases, even under the law of the land) sexual intercourse and relations—will be judged. I like the Message Bible's version of this: "Honor marriage, and guard the sacredness of sexual intimacy between wife and husband. God draws a firm line against casual and illicit sex" (Heb. 13:4).

Adulterers and fornicators will be judged. Adulterers are people who are already married to a spouse (husband or wife), but have sexual relations with someone other than their spouse. Fornicators are unmarried persons who have sexual relations, by definition, outside of the covenant of marriage. In this "hook-up" world there are so many broken lives, hearts, homes, bodies, and minds because this principle is considered irrelevant—that is judgment in itself. But also, I believe it means (on earth) that such persons do not and cannot ultimately prosper as the Lord desires, and they are not living in presence of God or the atmosphere of the His joy, peace, beauty, or grace; nor can they enter into His destiny for them. It also means such individuals will be judged eternally if they do not depart from these behaviors.

Just as a little aside here, Christ's first miracle was performed at the marriage in Cana. At that marriage, Jesus blessed the water and it became wine. There is deep spiritual significance to this event, and the Lord teaches us on many levels. But let's just think about this for a minute. Jesus didn't turn the water into wine and grace the couple with His presence at the "commitment ceremony of Cana" or the "adulterers' hotel room at Cana" or the "sex party at Cana." No, He blessed a marriage with His presence. His miracle carried a redemptive message of water to wine, the ordinary to the extraordinary. Wine represents the blood of Jesus whereby we are redeemed (set free from the power of sin, death, and hell), and it represents the Holy Spirit, the elevated joy of the presence of God in us. This happened at a *wedding*. "Cana" means "the nest." Here is where it all starts, the nest of family origins:

personalities, lives, prosperity, foundations, patterns of life, knowledge of God, love, self-worth—all the foundations.

Genesis 2:24 says, "Therefore shall a man leave his father and his mother, and shall cleave unto his wife: and they shall be one flesh." The marriage commitment talks of a man cleaving to his wife. The word *cleaving* in this context means to "join to" or "adhere to," affirmatively and consciously stay joined. It is also used in the sense of cleaving to the truth: Paul admonished the Romans to cleave to that which is good (Rom. 12:9). We can also extend this, full circle, to cleave to that which God has designed and declared as "good" such as the creation of man and woman. (It was "not good" for man to be alone, so He created woman to "cleave to.") The Word of God doesn't direct us to intentionally cleave to a girlfriend or boyfriend, long-term live-in partner, one night stand, hook-up, multiple sexual partners, self-stimulation, or porn, though strong attachments and bondages can certainly occur.

Marriage Reflects Christ's Love for His Church, and God's Relationship to His People in the Old and New Testament

In a way, all of us in Christ are in a "marriage" relationship—whether we are single or married. We are considered His bride, His body, birthed out of His side at the Cross. This contains the creative order, spiritual reproduction, governmental, covenantal, and divine order of God. While we are not in a physical relationship with Jesus, if we abide in Him, we will bear much fruit—spiritual reproduction (John 15:5). That also makes Him our husband, and we are to love and honor Him, and whether we are married on earth or not, keep our ultimate love, joy, and worship for Christ Himself, our Husband.

But here is what the Scripture says to those who are married in the natural: "Husbands, love your wives, even as Christ also loved the church, and gave Himself for it" (Eph. 5:25). Christ loving and giving Himself for the church was a huge order of sacrifice. God gave His Son, and allowed Jesus to be sacrificed so that multitudes of people who believed on Jesus Christ could experience eternal love and life.

That marriage should be compared to Christ's love for the church really draws a passionate picture of love, yet a holy one. too. Sacrifice, love, mercy, forgiveness, obedience, commitment, provision and protection, exclusivity (not adultery), pleasure, and joy are all parts of our relationship with Christ and part of the divine design to be reflected in marriage. This level of high living can only happen with committed people. By definition, people aren't going to spend long-term spiritual or emotional energy on casual sexual partners. Marriage, like all good relationships, requires the participants to give, forgive, change, and love, while the world encourages us to take, take, and take—and it is a fake existence.

Real life happens in any relational realm, with commitment, covenant, caring, forgiveness, faith, hope, and love. It also requires submitted and maturing people who understand these principles. The low maturity level in the society in which we live does not support marriage. It does not prepare young people for the divine pattern and covenant. You say that's OK, but is the devastation OK, the children aborted, the children left to themselves, abandoned, in the foster care system? Is the emotional, physical, and spiritual damage of promiscuity on men and women OK? Is it OK that people never grow up and become fully what God intended them to be by following the paths of obedience? Is the rampant spread of sexually transmitted diseases OK? If the Bible says something, it is not because it is just a good idea, it is because it is a God idea, and leads to eternal life. This is a huge challenge to the church of Jesus Christ to return to the old ways, the old patterns of holiness—which are really new. God is setting out a pattern of holiness and boundaries of living and channels of life. It is that simple. I am not talking about the world, but the people of God.

Here is a great verse for our times from the Message Bible:

Don't become so well-adjusted to your culture that
you fit into it without even thinking. Instead, fix your
attention on God. You'll be changed from the inside
out. Readily recognize what he wants from you, and
quickly respond to it. Unlike the culture around you,
always dragging you down to its level of immaturity,
God brings the best out of you, develops well-formed
maturity in you.

—ROMANS 12:2, THE MESSAGE

GOD LOVES PLEASURE IN MARRIAGE

Even Sarah, who was told at the age of ninety that she would
have a child, said, "Shall I have pleasure, my lord being old
also?" (Gen. 18:12). (Notice that Sarah calls Abraham "my lord"
as she is respectfully notes his position of honor. Abraham is
not her "old man." I'm not saying this needs to be our current approach, but honor should be bestowed by both parties.)
Does God want pleasure in marriage? Apparently the answer
was yes. God was in favor of it—He designed it so. Abraham
and Sarah supernaturally had a son named Isaac, which means
"laughter." God is in favor of romance, pleasure, and erotic love
in itself and for itself in the marriage covenant. Read the Song
of Solomon in the Bible, which is a love story between a man
and a woman but also a passionate representation of Christ
and His bride. This was pleasure for the sake of pleasure. He
delights in the way of a man with a woman (Prov. 30:19). God
invented the pleasure of sexuality, since He is the Creator. The
world and Satan can only manipulate God's invention. God
invented sex! Therefore, He gives the guidelines for its highest
expression and protection.

Yes, sexual pleasure can be extracted through sinful practices, just like opium can be extracted from poppies—but that
is living outside of the will of God. It turns people into com-
modities and objects. We can give a hundred examples here
of the fractured nature of sexual sin, but we all know this.
There is a lot of counterfeit living going on (as far as God is

concerned), like shattered parts of the glory that might have been. But people have always been driven by their own will, desires, brokenness, need, ignorance, lust, and disobedience as to what they want at any given moment for anything—nothing new with that.

Satan Hates Marriage

Satan hates marriage (Why wouldn't he? It was instituted of God with extravagant potential to bless the world), and the world is under his influence. Marriage started in paradise and will be brought to fullness in heaven, at the marriage supper of the Lamb. But for now, Ephesians 2:1–2 states, "And you hath he quickened [Jesus has made us alive to new life], who were dead in trespasses and sins; Wherein in time past ye walked according to the course of this world, according to the prince of the power of the air [airwaves—think of it, TV, Internet, radio, cell phones, any type of communication], the spirit that now worketh in the children of disobedience." The voices "out there" will try to convince people that their personal commitment is sufficient; it's OK to "shack up" with someone, or engage in sex without any boundaries, stream Internet porn, or seduce others to sin, and so forth. These societal ruling principles (and spiritual principalities) drive and direct people (including children), and provide sufficient justification to engage in any form of sexual sin. This is a lie, and is designed for *your* destruction. This is not love. God is love and if we love Him we will obey His commandments (John 14:15). (If you don't believe that there is real evil in this world or a real devil and influential demonic spirits, take it up with Jesus. He mentioned the topic a lot and took authority in the spirit realm.)

We already know that God will judge fornicators and adulterers, but other problems come to those who engage in sexual sin. Sin is not free. It always exacts wages, and the wages of sin is death (Rom. 6:23). That death may be a spiritual, emotional, or a physical one. Just to name a few areas where fornication brings spiritual, physical, or emotional death: sexual sin opens the door for sexually transmitted diseases, emotional bondage, transferences of unclean spirits of various types, sterility, increase in abortions, generational curses, and emotional damage. Certainly these results, among others, are the unattractive downside of sexual sin. But you say, many relationships I have had were lovely and enjoyable, the greatest time of my life. That may be in the natural realm and to the natural mind. Nevertheless, persisting in sexual sin ultimately blocks individuals from the promises, power, position, purpose, and presence of God. It's about destiny and eternity, holiness and wholeness. Hebrews 11:25 says that the pleasures of sin are only for a season. Yes, there is a season, but it ends. Whereas with the Lord, we have a steady covenant of life and blessings:

> Wherefore also we pray always for you, that our God would count you worthy of this calling, and fulfill all the good pleasure of his goodness, and the work of faith with power:
>
> —2 THESSALONIANS 1:11

> Thou wilt show me the path of life: in thy presence is fullness of joy; at thy right hand there are pleasures for evermore.
>
> —PSALM 16:11

Remember marriage, sexual capacity, and sexual expression were God's idea, not man's, nor the devil's. These are to be experienced, like anything else—money, employment, friendship—in the context that God the Creator designed. The devil didn't create people, their gender, sexuality, capacity for pleasure, reproductive capacity, or anything else for that matter. He's a user and a taker, a counterfeiter and a liar. The Lord created it all.

In this creative achievement God integrated His fabulous divine blessing and plan, which only could originate from Him—pleasure, unity, reproduction, stability, purpose, hope, companionship, life, warmth, a continuing heritage throughout generations, wealth, and eternity. Here's an extreme enjoyment with a divine and eternal purpose. How good can it get?

Therefore, when Satan ultimately tries to insert the lie of fornication or sexual sin into a people's minds, hearts, senses, and physical realm, he is not just trying to sabotage the institution of marriage. He is trying to sabotage all of life, including the love, plan, purpose, and position in God that God intended for individuals in marriage, as well as hindering people from eternal life and their divine destiny. What better way to get people to destroy themselves—turn one of their greatest gifts into a source of sin, and therefore, separation from God, openness to demonic influence, sickness, curses, confusion, and condemnation. Remember that Satan's temptations when acted upon cause us turn on ourselves in the end. The compromises and temptations we experience always come with the lure and lie of a better life, greater fulfillment, pleasure, satisfaction, and expression, as if God is withholding all of this; but in the end it is never so.

There is nothing in scripture to support same sex marriage. We all know this is a huge issue in our society. No matter how committed, a homosexual relationship cannot reflect the divine image and the biblical covenant of marriage—that's all. Please know that God loves persons who identify themselves as gay, and want to be gay, and those who experience same sex struggles, but don't want such struggles. The Father sent His Son Jesus to die for the sins (and brokenness) of the world—that's everyone, whether all people accept it or not. His death was an act of love. He took on the sin and brokenness of all human hearts on the cross, including homosexual acts, the homosexual condition, homosexual orientation, and homosexual fantasies, whether any individual receives His gift of love or not. Yet, even though all people are loved by Him, as a statement of the heart of God for His creation, it does not mean that it is His will for anyone to continue in any condition that is broken or any behavior that is sinful as described in Scripture, as I will discuss later. God's love is transformative.

His ultimate gift of love was for a purpose—so that we could come home to the Father and have eternal relationship with God. He provides an answer to all our identities, whether gay or straight, in the sacrifice of His Son, trading His life for ours. The Bible tells us that Jesus took our sins and our brokenness, and as we follow Him, there is *nothing* He cannot do. The path of holiness is worth it; wholeness is worth it, for all people, but it is not automatic or easy for anyone. With God all things are possible.

He also gives His children an identity as sons and daughters of God, in the image of His Son, through the Cross of Jesus Christ. There our old false lives and lies die, with our defenses and contradictions, and He gives us new life and truth in Him. In short, Jesus breaks through all false identities/selves to give us back a true one—Christ in us the hope of glory.

Accordingly, "homosexual marriage" is a contradiction in terms. The Living Word, Jesus, the One who defines life itself, has already defined marriage as between a man and woman—a covenantal relationship that is central to creation, confirms the image of God, and is a reflection of Christ's love for the church, as well as the Lord's relationship with His people as revealed in the Old Testament. It is an earthly relationship that is based in a divine relationship and the divine image. That is why it is not negotiable, even though many well-intentioned people want to redefine marriage and have succeeded in doing so in many places. Even if human law changes the definition of marriage, God has not. God is relational with His people to bear fruit, and so we have a marriage pattern—we are the bride of Christ, we are also His sons and daughters, friends and servants.

In the covenant of marriage, as defined by the Bible, the two become one; that is impossible in a homosexual relationship.

There can be massive bonding, but the unity of body, soul, and spirit (that is unity by the Holy Spirit) cannot happen because it is spiritually out of accord with Scripture and the Spirit of God, physically out of accord with the design of the body, and emotionally out of accord with wholeness. A person may have found the "perfect companion," "mate," or "life partner," but what is lost is the earthly relationship based on the divine relationship and image of God in Scripture. That can never be.

Yet, how do we approach gay persons or gay couples at our churches, or transsexuals or transgendered people for that matter? We let them know that God loves them deeply and passionately. We approach them with love, compassion, and healing and truth in the doses that can be received, like everyone else. All believers need the Holy Spirit to gently unravel their lives in His time and His way and release healing and a new way of living. Ministers are not the Holy Spirit; they are shepherds and servants ministering the truth and love of God—breaking it down, releasing the power and love, so people can receive. We as believers are all in process, and not in judgment. David said of the Lord, His gentleness has made me great (Ps. 18:35).

Raising Children

Marriage is God's highest and ordained relationship in which to have and raise children. His divine desire is that children be born into a family, with a committed husband and wife, father and mother—this is God's intended way for the child to be raised. Yes, parents fall short of this plan and not every marriage between man and woman reflects God's loving intent for the family, or is healthy, protective, good, loving, or holy. Sometimes it is better or safer for the children to be raised by one parent, relatives, or other caregivers. Many parents are deeply damaged, abusive, and cannot impart any sort of wholeness to the next generation. Also, some parents die or are absent for good reason. So, there are many ways that children innocently suffer or experience loss. Yet, that doesn't mean His plan and pattern are wrong. He designed the family and wants parents to be married for protection of the children, provision, godly examples and teaching, nurture and other reasons. The Bible is, among other things, a family story, which is set in the greater context of (His) story of creating a family. That is also why God wants to transform our souls and spirits as individuals, so we can live in His paths and patterns of life. This is actually stating the obvious and subject for another book.

The Old Testament describes the inherent rejection that comes with illegitimacy—something to think about and not to be taken lightly. Perhaps that is one reason that the Lord has great compassion on the fatherless—He wanted to make up the difference. Thankfully, the Cross of Jesus Christ nullifies all damage, curses, and losses under the law for those who come to the Cross—for He has taken the curse of the law. Remember the verse quoted at the beginning of this little book: "All the paths of the LORD are mercy and truth unto such as keep his covenant and his testimonies" (Ps. 25:10). There is a blessing that follows those who walk in His paths. This is for the protection and growth of children.

The Father has the same unfailing love for every person born on this planet, however they arrived here. He has plans, purposes and callings for every person, however they arrived here, and He does not come to condemn or judge the children, however they arrived here. Jesus Christ opened unlimited access to the throne of God for all people, no matter how or when they are born; for we are all saved by grace, not by our roots or how we arrived on this planet.

His highest plan is for children to have both parents—father and mother—in the home walking in a godly relationship. Each parent imparts his or her unique strengths and perspective to help the child grow. There are many sorrows that can come with lack of a parent in the home, for whatever reason. There is greater potential for poverty, low self-esteem, uncertain identities, neglect, violence, early pregnancy, criminal behavior, and abuse, among others. Children are simply more vulnerable without both parents.[2]

Jesus loves the little children. He died for them. If you were born on Planet Earth, God has a plan and purpose for your life. He even had a plan and purpose for the millions of children that were aborted. They were meant to be full human beings with desires, emotions, abilities, joys, and destinies that all the living have.

HUSBAND AND WIFE

The Book of Proverbs writes, Whoever finds a wife, finds a good thing, and obtains favor of the Lord (Prov. 18:22).

A wife is a good thing, and a wife and husband working together can help secure salvation and the blessings and promises of God for each other and for generations to come. God's favor is upon a man who finds a wife. That means that the man who finds a wife is on God's good side, and His loving eye is upon him. However, let's look at the scripture again: whoever "finds a wife," finds a good thing.

Note there is the implicit concept that marriage is a "resting place." Once that wife has been found, then the looking stops and the building of lives begins. Ideally, with somewhat morally or emotionally grounded people (hopefully spiritually too), the man (or woman) does not have to keep searching—in the most literal sense, what shall I do for companionship, what shall I do for sex, what shall I do for a family, who can I share my burdens with, how can I build my life—in the highest sense, the shopping stops when that "good thing" has been found. Furthermore, because the married couple becomes "one flesh," something new has been created—and whatever God joins together let no man put asunder. The Bible says that there is a rest for the people of God (Heb. 4:9).

There is no rest in fornication, there is no rest in adultery, there is no rest spiritually in homosexuality, and there is no rest in sexual lust—in fact lust just drives a person more and more. It has a repetitive, compulsive, but empty quality. These are inherently broken behaviors. Basically, all sin is a disruption of the divine pattern as ordained by heaven. Thankfully, the blood of Jesus interrupts sin, putting things back in order again with the Word of God and the Holy Spirit.

Marriage is a covenant. Marriage is a covenantal relationship established by God as early as the Garden of Eden—in fact the first covenantal relationship between humans, and repeated in the Old and New Testaments, as I wrote earlier. It is foundational to the stability of human life on this planet. God placed man and woman in a context where love could grow, pleasure could be deepened, life could flourish, and they could be fruitful and multiply, where people could build in love. Isn't that the best way to build? When we depart from this covenant and pattern, there will be sorrow.

Male and female bodies are designed for each other for all the purposes described earlier—sexual expression, unity, pleasure, creating children, and others. Men and women don't have to "take turns" for sexual climax, they have the capacity built in to do it together—it seems like a God idea to me, adding to the unity and pleasure of the couple. Their spirits can be in unity, especially for those in Christ, and hopefully their emotions and gifting can complement each other for even greater unity and expansion. There is no conflict with the Holy Spirit.

BOOKENDS OF SPIRITUAL HISTORY ON MARRIAGE—THE COVENANT OF MARRIAGE

I just want to clarify something here. The Lord established the covenant of marriage in the Garden of Eden. Man and woman were in a state of innocence at that time. Before sin entered the human race, the Lord had set the pattern: one man, one woman, one covenant. Some people argue that not long thereafter men had multiple wives, as well as other sexual partners—it was quite common and therefore acceptable. Historically, there was a departure from the pattern set up in the Garden after sin entered the human race, but that does not mean it was God's original or final intent. His original and final intent is declared by Jesus Christ. Whatever happened historically, Jesus once again clearly affirmed and confirmed the original covenant of marriage between one man and one woman in Mark 10:6–9 over 2,000 years ago in the new covenant. While we can never go back to the innocence of the Garden and its glory, we can move forward to glory of holiness, which Jesus introduces through His life, death, and resurrection.

VIRGINITY AND COVENANT

Just as a final thought, every covenant is established by the words of the covenant including the terms and the oath of the covenant, the seal of the covenant and the blood of the covenant. Let's see how this works in the covenant of marriage. This may seem very old fashioned to twenty-first century readers, but the old truths and the old paths have the new life because they carry the vitality of the divine blessing.

> Thus says the LORD: "Stand in the ways and see, And ask for the old paths, where the good way is, And walk in it; Then you will find rest for your souls."
> —JEREMIAH 6:16, NKJV

The oath of the covenant on the natural level is equal to the marriage vows, and on the spiritual level, the promises of God for obedience in this area. The seal of the covenant is the joining as one flesh and the seal of God on the marriage, but it also has to do with the very physical act of breaking the seal of virginity, where there is blood, that original seal of innocence and purity, to enter into the seal of holy matrimony and intimacy. It is meant to be a deep, holy, and exclusive communion (body and blood) between husband and wife. Is virginity to be honored? Yes. The Lord profoundly created marriage with this seal/oath/blood covenant.

> But you are a chosen generation, a royal priesthood, a holy nation, His own special people, that you may

proclaim the praises of Him who called you out of darkness into His marvelous light; who once were not a people but are now the people of God, who had not obtained mercy but now have obtained mercy.

—1 PETER 2:9–10, NKJV

Let us not base our actions on the level of immaturity and compromise of the world. Does this all seem impossible to you, and outside of your experience? Yes, it is impossible without the grace of God and knowledge of Jesus Christ in the inner man and the transforming power of the Holy Spirit, as we will see in the next segment. The way is narrow. Is marriage some magical place where everything is right, just, perfect, and happy? Should all people desire or aspire to marriage? No, but it is a God-ordained place to work out your salvation with another person with potential for life, love, and joy. The Bible tells us that by grace are we saved, but I think we are saved not just in the beginning of our journey when we come into relationship with Jesus Christ; we are saved every day, in and out, up and down, night and day. We need His grace in all things and at all times.

Part II

SEX OUTSIDE OF MARRIAGE

*Any Kind, Any Way, With Anyone—Invitation to
Sorrow and Open Door to Consequences*

*You know the guidelines we laid out for you from the
Master Jesus. God wants you to live a pure life. Keep
yourselves from sexual promiscuity. Learn to appre-
ciate and give dignity to your body, not abusing it, as is
so common among those who know nothing of God.*
—1 Thessalonians 4:2–5, the message

*Furthermore then we beseech you, brethren, and exhort
you by the Lord Jesus, that as ye have received of us
how ye ought to walk and to please God, so ye would
abound more and more. For ye know what commandments we gave you by the Lord Jesus. For this is the will
of God, even your sanctification, that ye should abstain
from fornication: That every one of you should know
how to possess his vessel in sanctification and honor.*
—1 Thessalonians 4:1–4

THIS IS HOW we walk and please God—so you will
abound. The word *abound* means increase, abundantly
supplied. This is a commandment given even by the
Lord Jesus Christ, so we would abound or increase more and
more. This is the will of God. There is no doubt about it; you
should abstain or not engage in fornication during the process
leading to sanctification, or the process of becoming holy like

Him. Possess your body with a holy dignity. Seems like a new concept in our society, but remember that we are a holy people and our bodies are the temple of the Holy Spirit. God gives us the truth of the Word of God, so we can obey the Lord with regard to relationships and receive His blessings as we walk in obedience. I am not saying that believers don't make mistakes here, or get off track, have failures, or even agree with these scriptures, but I just want the readers of this book to see what the Bible actually says, and the blessings or consequences of agreeing or disagreeing with Scripture, the higher call of a life in Christ. Some will receive it, and some will not. I didn't make this up. While, as the translation above says, this (fornication) is common among those who know nothing of God, when we do know of a holy, loving God, we understand the boundaries He establishes for our good and ultimate blessing, not to mention glorifying Him.

You are already abounding if someone commits to you for life. You may say that there are many happy and prosperous couples who are not married, or people enjoying life and sexual activities who are not even thinking about marriage. So what? You can gain the whole world and lose Jesus and your soul. Everything a person can desire or possess does not add up to the destiny we have in God gained by humble obedience. Remember Proverbs 10:22 (NLT): "The blessing of the LORD makes a person rich, and he adds no sorrow with it." James 1:17 (NLT): "Whatever is good and perfect comes to us from God above, who created all heaven's lights. Unlike them, he never changes or casts shifting shadows."

Also, there is a difference between being a holy people and "of the world."

> Wherefore come out from among them, and be ye separate, saith the Lord.
>
> —2 Corinthians 6:17

Because we have these promises, dear friends, let us cleanse ourselves from everything that can defile our body or spirit. And let us work toward complete purity because we fear God.

—2 Corinthians 7:1, nlt

Adulterers and adulteresses! Do you not know that friendship with the world is enmity with God? Whoever therefore wants to be a friend of the world makes himself an enemy of God.

—James 4:4, nkjv

I agree with Scripture, as stated in Psalm 144:15, that no matter what pleasures the world may have, "Happy is that people, that is in such a case: yea, happy is that people, whose God is the Lord." And Psalm 84:10 (nlt): "A single day in your courts is better than a thousand anywhere else! I would rather be a gatekeeper in the house of my God than live the good life in the homes of the wicked."

The biblical term for sex outside of marriage defined in Scripture is *fornication*. It comes from the Greek word *porneia* from which we get the word *pornography* today. In the Bible it can mean unlawful lust and sinful sexual activity.

It is illicit or unlawful sex, sex outside of the marriage relationship according to Scripture. The Lord states this for our holiness, increase, blessing, favor, and happiness. There is an ease and casualness, not to mention abusiveness, in which people enter into sexual relationships or have sexual experiences outside of marriage in our twenty-first-century world. This casual regard for sex would make it seem that fornication or a sexual encounter or experience is not a big deal. But it is a source of much brokenness and damage, and separates a person from God, who is the source of life. It is a big deal to God because it is against the creative and divine pattern He set up when He created this world. Break the Word and it will break you, as others have said.

"Fornication" can include the following: Sex outside of divinely defined marriage, between man and woman, male and male, female and female (in other words it includes homosexual/lesbian sexual relationships), prostitution, adultery, child sexual abuse, incest, and combinations that the human mind can think of. We also have to consider the impact of fantasy sex (porn, erotic experiences, or masturbation, since fornication starts in our hearts [desire and imagination], as Jesus says), and other forms of sexual stimulation. Our "heart" has a broad definition in the Greek. It includes the soul or mind, as it is the fountain and seat of the thoughts, passions, desires, appetites, affections, purposes, endeavors; of the understanding, the faculty and seat of the intelligence.[1]

Marriage is the divine model. That doesn't mean that great, holy, anointed, or even good people are married; it just means that they have entered into a God-ordained pattern, whether they realize it or not. Many abuses and crimes may happen in the context of marriage, but we have to separate the sinfulness and brokenness of people from the source of the pattern, like anything else. Abuses happen at places of employment, but that doesn't mean we shouldn't work. Abuses happen on the freeway, but that doesn't mean we shouldn't drive. That which comes from the distractions, idolatry, lust, ignorance, brokenness, sinful willfulness of the human heart, or even well meaning passion or love out of the will of God, is going to have a cost and consequence. Even though not all marriages work, and the home can be the place of many disasters, marriage itself is still honorable, and a pattern set by God.

WHAT DOES THE BIBLE SAY ABOUT FORNICATION?

Jesus said: "For from within, out of the heart of men, proceed evil thoughts, adulteries, fornications, murders, thefts...all these evil things come from within, and defile the man" (Mark 7:21–23). Notice that Jesus says "fornications," plural. Jesus tells us that fornication (sinful sexual activity and experiences as described above) starts with the interior or heart of a person and moves to evil thought and/or physical expression.

Where does Jesus say fornication begins? It starts in our hearts. Fornication is listed as something "evil" by Jesus Himself, and it "defiles" or makes a person spiritually unclean. *Defile* actually means to render unholy, unclean, to stain, contaminate morally, besmear, as with mud or filth, to make a spot.

"Evil thoughts" can happen without engaging in actual sexual intercourse or physical skin on skin experiences. The thought life includes what people permit, meditate upon, or expose themselves to, some common current examples being "sexting," porn, virtual sex, strippers, erotic images and the like. These may be preliminary steps for actions out of the will of God, but even in themselves, are defiling.

The Scriptures state: "Know ye not that ye are the temple of God, and that the Spirit of God dwelleth in you? If any man defiles the temple of God, him shall God destroy; for the temple of God is holy, which temple ye are" (1 Cor. 3:16–17).

Your body is the temple of God. You are carrying the Holy Spirit in you. The Bible speaks clearly here; if any person defiles or makes unclean the temple of God, him God will destroy.

The Scriptures also state:

> Know ye not that the unrighteous shall not inherit the kingdom of God? [Don't you know that wrong-doers will have no share in God's kingdom?] Be not deceived: neither fornicators, nor idolaters, nor adulterers, nor effeminate, nor abusers of themselves with mankind, nor thieves, nor covetous, nor drunkards, nor revilers, nor extortionists, *shall inherit the kingdom of God.*
>
> —1 Corinthians 6:9–11, emphasis added

Don't you know that those who do wrong will have no share in the Kingdom of God? Don't fool yourselves. Those who indulge in sexual sin, who are idol worshipers, adulterers, male prostitutes, homosexuals, thieves, greedy people, drunkards, abusers, and swindlers—none of these will have a share in the Kingdom of God. There was a time when some of you were just like that, but now your sins have been washed away, and you have been set apart for God. You have been made right with God because of what the Lord Jesus Christ and the Spirit of our God have done for you.

—1 Corinthians 6:9–11, nlt

And such were some of you, [Some of you once belonged to these categories] *but you are washed,* [but you're your sins are washed away]…*sanctifi*ed, [you became Christ's people]…*justified in the name of the Lord Jesus, and by the Spirit of our God* [and He has accepted you because of what the Lord Jesus and the Spirit of our God have done for you.]" What is Paul saying here under the inspiration of the Holy Spirit?

First, fornicators, adulterers, and a list of others engaged in sexual and *other sins* (though we will concentrate on the sexual sins here) *will not inherit the kingdom of God.* A person may see the kingdom of God, may want the kingdom of God, or even have something of a relationship with God, but the fornicator and the rest on the list will not *possess* the kingdom of God. They will not be in a position of sonship to receive and inherit it, or have access to its blessings. The kingdom will be elusive and out of reach. Just as the Israelites wandered around for forty years after being liberated from Egypt—they knew God had something better for them, but because of their disobedience, complaining, idolatry, and other extremely poor attitudes and actions, they never possessed it. They had many promises, God had great intentions for them, and He was still with them, but they missed it—one of the reasons, among many, being that they engaged in fornication (1 Cor. 10:1–11).

What is the issue here? Yes, Christians stumble, get drunk, become greedy, commit adultery, steal, covet, and so forth. But the list above of those who will not inherit the kingdom of God is comprised of people who have fundamentally decided to stay in that way of life and reject the will of God as stated in Scripture. God is looking for hearts that will be molded and humbled before Him, willing to submit to a process of transformation.

Here's another way to look at it scripturally: Joseph, the favored son of Jacob, described in the Book of Genesis, had a great destiny which the Lord showed him in his two dreams. After being sold into slavery by his brothers, he ended up in the house of an Egyptian named Potiphar who was an officer of Pharaoh, a captain of the guard (Gen. 39). While he lived in Potiphar's house, Joseph did a great job handling Potiphar's lands and home. Potiphar's wife wanted to have an illicit sexual relationship with him. Joseph *could have* had sex with this woman, and all would have been great for him—running the place, having all his needs met, and having sex with Potiphar's wife—but he would have stayed in Potiphar's house and never possessed the promises of greatness for his own life, his own house, his own people, and his own children. His true identity would have been lost as well as his destiny. His obedience or disobedience would have an impact for eternity, even the coming of the Messiah. Wisely he chose not to sin against God (Gen. 39:9). The New Testament says, flee fornication (1 Cor. 6:18). Joseph ran because he had the integrity of God in his heart. Consequently he was imprisoned because of the false accusations of Potiphar's wife, but the trouble vaulted him from the king's prison to the king's palace. Second Corinthians 4:17–18 (NLT) says, "For our present troubles are quite small and won't last very long. Yet they produce for us an immeasurably great glory that will last forever! So we don't look at the troubles we can see right now; rather, we look forward to what we have not yet seen. For the troubles we see will soon be over, but the joys to come will last forever." Potiphar's wife doesn't even have a name in the story. The wicked are blown away like chaff (Ps. 1:4).

Second, don't be deceived. Don't listen to the lies out there (remember the prince of the power of the air[waves], Satan, the spirit that now works in the children of disobedience [Eph. 2:2]) through your boyfriend, girlfriend, or yourself, hook-up, TV, Internet, the movies, the degradation of contemporary media and entertainment, amplified with drugs and alcohol. The promises of God work with obedience. We cannot expect the Lord's protection, blessing, or favor ultimately by continuing in such sins. Sure the "Man Upstairs," as some people refer to the Lord, helps people who don't even know Him and are certainly not committed to Him; but to live in God's continued favor, protection, blessing, and presence is another level of life. God loves us unconditionally through His great offer of love on the cross, but He does not bless us unconditionally.

There are some blessings that are released to the just and unjust. The rain comes to the just and unjust; the sun shines on the just and unjust; life, gifts, and talents are built into us, the just and unjust. We can all remember how the Lord sustained us even in times of disobedience. But the promises of God, our destiny in God, and the ongoing presence of God require obedience, willingness, submission, and commitment. David prayed in Psalm 51:11, "Cast me not away from thy presence; and take not thy Holy Spirit from me." If we lose the presence of God, we lose everything. God is not trying to constrict and restrict us; He is showing a higher life and destiny, and a deeper and more meaningful experience, if done His way.

However, there is a great promise with 1 Corinthians 6:9–11: Those who engage in sexual sin, including homosexuality, or drunkards or thieves, and so forth (notice God isn't "picking on" those who engage in sexual sin) *don't have to stay that way*—the power of the Holy Spirit, the name of Jesus, is more than able to deliver us and wash us and make us holy. Paul writes: "Such *were some of you*" (v. 11, emphasis added).

This is past tense. No person has to stay in a sinful pattern unless they want to. This does not mean that believers do not struggle at times, but He whom the Son sets free is free indeed. *Nothing is unchangeable or impossible with God.* Liberation requires a struggle, but isn't freedom worth it? Don't all victories require battles?

It is going to take the process of repentance and forgiveness, healing and restoration to cleanse away the sinful patterns of behavior, the broken condition of our souls and negative and selfish thought patterns, but it is worth it. You know, God really blesses us when He calls "sin," "sin." That gives us tremendous guidance, and confidence that He (and only He) can cleanse and release us from sin, from brokenness we have experienced and many other limitations to a full life in Christ. He identifies the problem and provides the solution—Jesus Christ in us. He also gives us guidance. "This is the way, walk ye in it" (Isa. 30:21).

A lot of people say, this is who I am and all I know. What about who He is, and what He can do in your life? Let Him do His work in you and through you. Who is God after all, you or Him? This is a process; it is not instantaneous. It is recognizing Him as Lord of all and being reborn by His Spirit. If you have never done this, the prayers at the end of this book start with the prayer of salvation. Pray this now even if you don't finish the book today.

When we walk in faith, we accept His Word and receive the forgiveness, deliverance, healing, and restoration the Lord provides. On the other hand, those who reject Him and His Word consequently degrade their own lives. Jesus was distressed with the Jews in His day because they rejected Him. It wasn't just a "personal thing" of not being loved; it stopped the flow of blessings and favor He dearly wanted to give to them. He wept over a city that rejected Him because they had rejected God Himself and the kingdom of heaven. Their hearts were hardened so they could not believe and therefore be healed (John 12:39–40). The Lord says in Jeremiah 13:17,

"But if ye will not hear it, my soul shall weep in secret places for your pride; and mine eye shall weep sore, and run down with tears, because the Lord's flock is carried away captive." Jeremiah's heart (the Lord's heart) was broken because the people of God in that day went their own way because of their pride, for it was the path of captivity.

But if we know *what* is the *will* of *God* through the *Word* of *God*, and accept the *ways* of God, then we know *where* the *power* of *God* can be applied for our cleansing, healing, and restoration by faith. "Wholeness" flows from "holiness." Holiness first flows from God's forgiveness of our sins day by day, based on our acknowledgement of the truth and our sin, leading to personal repentance. The door is now open for the kingdom and power of God in our lives over all the power of the enemy through the blood of Jesus. Continual sanctification (being made holy) and wholeness occurs as we are cleansed in our spirits and renewed by the working of the Holy Spirit in our minds, including our thought processes, will and emotions daily. (See Romans 12:1–2.) As the sin issues are taken care of, the Lord can do a deeper work of deliverance, healing and restoration, leading to wholeness. The power of the Cross can release us from patterns of sin, destructive emotions, shame, sadness, guilt, and pain, demonic oppression, generational curses, soul ties, negative core beliefs, gaps in growth and maturation, and any other hindrances to our fullness as human beings created by God and recreated in the image of Jesus Christ through the power of the resurrection by the Holy Spirit. When we are cleansed from sin and its results our hearts can be healed from the damage of sin, and we become "whole" as an ongoing process.

The Scriptures say, "The body is *not* for fornication, but for the Lord; and the Lord for the body" (1 Cor. 6:13, emphasis added). How is the body to be used? Not for fornication, but for the Lord. You are His temple and home here on earth. If you owned a house and someone rented your house, would you be pleased if they allowed it to become unclean, broke the windows, damaged the appliances and utility lines, knocked holes in the walls, and invited their friends to live there? Probably not. You are God's house. He lives in you. Fornication breaks fellowship with the Master, and actually the body of Christ, and defiles the whole person.

> Don't you realize that your bodies are actually parts of Christ? Should a man take his body, which belongs to Christ, and join it to a prostitute? Never! And don't you know that if a man joins himself to a prostitute, he becomes one body with her? For the Scriptures say, "The two are united into one." But the person who is joined to the Lord becomes one spirit with him.
> —1 CORINTHIANS 6:15–17, NLT

He wants us to yield our members as "instruments of righteousness," not sin.

> Run away from sexual sin! No other sin so clearly affects the body as this one does. For sexual immorality is a sin against your own body. Or don't you know that your body is the temple of the Holy Spirit, who lives in you and was given to you by God? You do not belong to yourself, for God bought you with a high price. So you must honor God with your body.
> —1 CORINTHIANS 6:18–20, NLT

Some things to note from these scriptures:

Our bodies belong to the Lord—they are members of Christ (1 Cor. 6:15). When a person engages in sex, he or she takes Jesus with them. Wouldn't the Holy Spirit be grieved if that body was used for fornication? Sexual relations are so fundamental and basic, and God's commandments so clear in Scripture, that it is hard to rationalize disobedience in this area. The Bible says in 1 Corinthians 10:13, there is no temptation such as is "common to man." That means no one is an exception and whatever justification (love, passion, ignorance, "special needs" of the moment, day, season, or year) we can give for our actions is not new and exclusive. There is nothing new under the sun (Eccles. 1:9).

You are bought with a price (1 Cor. 6:20)—the blood of Jesus; don't drag His sacrifice into a sinful and compromised situation.

You become one flesh with someone with whom you have sex. That is why the sexual bond is so hard to break and has so many consequences.

The Lord tells us to *run from fornication*. Run, because if you hang around long enough, there will be plenty of reasons to rationalize sinning. Once the sexual urge kicks in, it is hard to stop.

Fornication is a sin against your own body. Therefore, it usually has results and consequences in your own body.

Your body is to glorify God. You are not your own anymore.

You can't glorify God in your spirit if your body is dishonoring Him.

The Lord is very clear in all this. He is in support of marriage. He designed it. Everything else is outside of His will.

The bonds of covenant are broken everywhere in our society. It is like a moral and spiritual nuclear blast. The Bible says: "He [Jesus] upholds all things by the word of His power" (Heb. 1:3). Jesus holds together every atom. But when that word of His power is broken, everything blows apart. Broken lives and broken bodies are strewn about on the emotional, moral, and spiritual landscape, and most do not have the knowledge and power to put their lives back together again. In the Book of Malachi in the Old Testament, the prophet was grieved at the many broken covenants in his day also; covenants of the priesthood, marriage, between brothers and between generations. It was going to take the Messenger of the Covenant (Jesus Christ), then as now, to put all the pieces back together again in divine order for His blessing and His purposes.

Why Is It So Hard to Break Sexual Ties?

As Paul writes in the scriptures above, you become *one* with the person you have sex with.

Let's talk about soul ties for a moment.

Sexual relations create a unique bond. It is a building block to bring a unique happiness and unity to the married couple. This bond is intended to grow and be nurtured in marriage. Outside of marriage, a bond is still created, but it does not have the favor, protection, and position of marriage in God; and when it is *broken*, you still feel a connection with the other person. When there is a tearing away from the other person, souls are fragmented.

These soul ties can exist whether a person consents to sex or not. A molested child or victim of rape can experience a negative connection with the abuser, potentially for a lifetime. The soul tie must be broken, and deliverance and healing ministered, so the victim can be free of the pain, guilt, shame, anger, self-hatred, and other emotional fallout from the experience, as well as entrance of demonic spirits and transferences of demonic spirits. In addition the molestation can freeze and traumatize the emotions of the child that can hinder development. The victim experiences emotional trauma and death at that point to one degree or another. The shame that results becomes a tightly sealed box that can limit the child for life. The same occurs with rape.

Most people's souls in this society have been tied and pulled apart, therefore fragmented many times, and that is one reason why commitment in marriage is so difficult and people are emotionally desensitized. Sadly, some people engage in sexual experiences because that is what everyone is doing. That is how to be a part of the action, or it is an important source of pleasure to which they are entitled (fueled by drugs and alcohol), not to mention the driving lust and brokenness involved, intersecting with God-created natural desires. The roots of this attitude are very deep, and do not in any way reflect true manhood or womanhood or anything else for that matter.

Nobody said it isn't enjoyable. If sex wasn't enjoyable the human race probably would be extinct. But Paul summarized the current prevalent attitude and reversed priorities about 2,000 years ago: People are "lovers of pleasures" more than lovers of God (2 Tim. 3:4). Our society reinforces and romanticizes this view. Our cultural patterns accept it as "normal" and demand no boundaries. Desire, "love," and need rule. Casual sex is no big deal—it is casual. Children are sexualized at an early age, and so become the new consumers of the products, entertainment, and eventually, brokenness of our day. This casual sexual attitude and all its grievous results continue generationally. It is not normal to Jesus, who is the Living Word, and the pattern for living.

At the end of this Scripture study, there are prayers to break soul ties particularly to persons and images (even objects) in the sexual realm. These are a starting point. Break these ties and ask the Lord to restore your soul. This will help free you to be healed and focused on the things of God and be able to enter into a true relationship in marriage, if that is what you desire (or a deeper and more honest relationship, if you are married), or most importantly a true relationship with the Lord, yourself, and others. You will have greater freedom to walk in this life as the Lord commands and desires. If a person carries all these soul ties into marriage, commitment will be much more difficult. If you are married, repent and break ties with partners in other sexual encounters, experiences, relationships, places, porn, and things. Many people have the attitude that casual sex is no big deal—but why are they having such a hard time staying in or even wanting a committed relationship? Perhaps it is because of fragmented souls and the continual degradation of what God intended to be holy. And why is marriage itself becoming more and more exceptional and irrelevant to our society?

Also, people enter into many ungodly covenants—in short,

compromises, agreements, and trade-offs that are not of God—and these transfer unclean spirits between people and create bondages. Perhaps there are promises and commitments out of the will of God that you entered into (in any realm). Such ungodly covenants must be repented of, renounced, and broken as well, spirits expelled, and healing released. Again, this book is talking about spiritual principles. You may say to yourself, I have never heard of anything like this. What does this have to do with me? Folks, there is a spiritual dimension to all our activities. Everything we do echoes in eternity—even something as simple as giving a cup of cold water to a person in the name of Jesus, or saying a lie to a stranger.

When we walk according to the law of the Spirit of life in Christ Jesus we are free from the law of sin and death (Rom. 8:1–2). But if we walk according to the flesh or in disobedience, whether we know it or not, we become subject to the law of sin and death. It isn't just, "Well, I did this for a while, and there were no consequences." There are spiritual enforcers on both sides of the spirit realm, and we reap a crop of whatever we sow. When Jesus died on the cross, His broken body and shed blood interrupted and overcame the massive destructiveness caused by sin—sickness, grief, sorrow, curses, eternity in hell, death, demonic power, the power of the world, the flesh, and the devil. When we accept the fullness of His sacrifice, we obtain the benefits of the new covenant and eternal life. When we reject His sacrifice, the law of sin and death is at work.

Many people have the attitude that sexual relations are just "recreational," and that the other person is just an object for momentary pleasure, or they travel to a quick and easy escape into pornography. Basically people are disobedient without caring. It is often difficult to do things God's way in any realm—it requires us to grow and have patience and faith. It requires dying to the flesh, which is not pleasant, and sometimes persecution and serious testing (which tests the Word in us), but it reaps the peaceable fruits of righteousness. And here is where we throw our lives down before Him, "to know

Him, the power of His resurrection, and the fellowship of His sufferings, being made conformable to His death" (Phil. 3:10). Yes, brothers and sisters, the fellowship of His sufferings exists too, when our flesh dies (i.e., does not rule our decisions), and we just do it His way because it is the "highway of holiness" (Isa. 35:8). The Lord means that for all people, whatever their direction to the Cross. God is in the business of creating and recreating people in His image; that is His divine pattern and plan.

Most people don't even know any better, but God did not design human beings simply to be stimulated, or receptacles or releasers of body fluids; nor did the Lord ordain life without His holy dimension—no matter how great. God has a much higher design for life—one that is rooted in heaven itself—on earth as it is in heaven—and is a very picture of Christ's love for His church. When His truth is ignored, there is still toll on a person's emotions and body. Those who engage in recreational sex and immorality (including porn and sexual experiences—live or electronic) become desensitized to godly love and truth, and become separated from God. In the end you cannot be the person God created you to be. You can gain the whole world and lose the destiny the Lord desires for you, the very purpose of your life. Even if you have a committed partner or significant other and are not promiscuous, it is still out of the will of God.

I like these verses as expressed in the Message Bible:

> God honored the Master's body by raising it from the grave. He'll treat yours with the same resurrection power. Until that time, remember that your bodies are created with the same dignity as the Master's body. You wouldn't take the Master's body off to a whorehouse, would you? I should hope not." [*Listen to this:*] There's more to sex than mere skin on skin. Sex is as much spiritual mystery as physical fact. As written in Scripture, "The two become one." Since

we want to become spiritually one with the Master, we must not pursue the kind of sex that avoids commitment and intimacy, leaving us more lonely than ever—the kind of sex that can never "become one." There is a sense in which sexual sins are different from all others. In sexual sin we violate the sacredness of our own bodies, these bodies that were made for God-given and God-modeled love, for "becoming one" with another. Or didn't you realize that your body is a sacred place, the place of the Holy Spirit? Don't you see that you can't live however you please, squandering what God paid such a high price for? The physical part of you is not some piece of property belonging to the spiritual part of you. God owns the whole works. So let people see God in and through your body.

—1 Corinthians 6:14–20, the message

The question is, will we follow a lower life or higher life? The Amplified Bible Version renders Mark 8:35 as follows: "For whoever wants to save his [higher, spiritual, eternal] life, will lose it [the lower, natural, temporal life which is lived only on earth]; and whoever gives up his life [which is lived only on earth] for My sake and the Gospel's will save it [his higher, spiritual life in the eternal kingdom of God]."

Any sinful practices—whatever they are—lead to "non-being" because they are in flight from the will of the Creator as revealed by the truth of the Word of God. We can all live lies, or park ourselves in lies for a period of time, but the only way to move forward is to acknowledge the truth, and be empowered by the Holy Spirit.

Further, who can make godly decisions when involved sexually with a person? How many people have thrown away fortunes, futures, and family, as well as health and other blessings, because of sexual encounters or relationships out of the will of God? With sexual relations there is not only a physical connection, but a spiritual, emotional, and mental connection leading to transference of feelings, spirits, and thoughts. The thief comes to steal, kill, and destroy. Thankfully, the Lord forgives and restores our souls, but sometimes it is a long way back and sometimes damage cannot be reversed.

> For sexual immorality is a sin against your own body.
> —1 Corinthians 6:18, nlt

What Are Some of the Consequences of Sexual Sin As Stated in Scriptures?

We have described some of these already:

- God will destroy those who defile the temple of God (the body).

- You sin against your own body, and therefore bring to your body the results of those sins.

- The sexually immoral will not inherit the kingdom of heaven.

There's more: (Now I want you to know what the Word of God says—I didn't make this up. It seems a bit harsh to the natural mind—everyone's doing it, this is how it is, this is who I am, I enjoy this, what's wrong with this, and so forth. But I want to emphasize that we are dealing with a spiritual truth and there are consequences in the natural realm.)

Plagues

"Neither let us commit fornication as some of them committed, and fell in one day three and twenty thousand" (1 Cor. 10:8) ["And we must not engage in sexual immorality as some of them did, causing 23,000 of them to die in one day," nlt]. This is speaking of the Israelites who sinned in the wilderness due to fornication. A plague fell on them.

> Come out of her, my people, that ye be not partakers
> of her sins, and that ye receive not of her plagues.
> —Revelation 18:4

In speaking of the sins of Babylon, God called His people to come out of Babylon's sins, so they would not receive the plagues that would come on Babylon. Babylon represents spiritual harlotry (prostitution) in the Bible, basically a degrading departure from God. It means loving and giving yourself to everything but God.

Read Deuteronomy chapter 28 to see the results of disobedience. Sexually transmitted diseases are rampant in the world. They wipe out whole nations, cause sterility, premature births or miscarriages, infect children, leave orphans, and drain the resources of families, individuals, and governments. Can this be good and godly, lots of fun, worth the cost, reflective of the divine?

The wrath of God

> For this ye know, that no whoremonger [same word used above], nor unclean person, nor covetous man, who is an idolater, hath any inheritance in the kingdom of Christ and of God. Let no man deceive you with vain [empty, worthless, deceptive—"I love you," or "it doesn't mean anything," "it's just sex"] words, for because of these things [fornication, uncleanness, etc.] cometh the wrath of God upon the children of disobedience. Be not ye therefore partakers with them.
>
> —EPHESIANS 5:5–7

Here's another translation:

> You can be sure that no immoral, impure, or greedy person will inherit the Kingdom of Christ and of God. For a greedy person is really an idolater who worships the things of this world. Don't be fooled by those who try to excuse these sins, for the terrible anger of God comes upon all those who disobey him. Don't participate in the things these people do. For though your hearts were once full of darkness, now

you are full of light from the Lord, and your behavior should show it!

—Ephesians 5:5–8, nlt

Some people wonder why nothing ever works out in their lives. Could it be that they are spiritually committing suicide by their own sexual behavior? The anger of God comes on the children of disobedience. His blessings are not intended for those who habitually, and as a matter of intentional practice, break His covenant and Word. I've prayed for a lot of people, and seen the effects.

Fornication and adultery lead to poverty and shame

For by means of a whorish woman [one engaged in ungodly sexual intercourse] a man is brought to a piece of bread: and the adulteress will hunt for the precious life. Can a man take fire in his bosom, and his clothes not be burned? Can one go upon hot coals, and his feet not be burned? So he that goeth in to his neighbor's wife; whosoever toucheth her shall not be innocent.

—Proverbs 6:26–29

Whoso commiteth adultery with a woman lacketh understanding: he that doeth it destroyeth his own soul. A wound and dishonor shall he get, and he reproach [shame] shall not be wiped away.

—verses 32–33

These commands and this teaching will keep you from the immoral woman, from the smooth tongue of an adulterous woman. Don't lust for her beauty. Don't let her coyness seduce you. For a prostitute will bring you to poverty, and sleeping with another man's wife may cost you your very life. Can a man scoop fire into his lap and not be burned? Can he walk on hot coals and not blister his feet? So it is with

the man who sleeps with another man's wife. He who
embraces her will not go unpunished.

—PROVERBS 6:24–29, NLT

Fornication leads to death and hell

The house of the "strange woman" or "strange man" is the
way to hell, going down to the chambers of death. Many have
been wounded and *strong men [and women] have been slain
by her [him]* (Prov. 7:26–27).

The woman or man who engages in sex outside of marriage
is on the way to hell and death. That seducing spirit coming
through the "strange woman" or man is meant to destroy.
Many are wounded.—*strong men, not weak ones—and have
been slain.*

Sexual sin can lead to the grave and disgrace

Here are some consequences: Loss of wealth and laboring
to gain someone else's wealth (see the scriptures below).
Committed marriage can lead to extension of life and prosperity, for it is God's building block for society; couple that
with obedience regarding money, and the only direction is up.
(That is another study.)

> The lips of an immoral woman are as sweet as honey,
> and her mouth is smoother than oil. But the result
> is as bitter as poison, sharp as a double-edged sword.
> Her feet go down to death; her steps lead straight to
> the grave. For she does not care about the path to life.
> She staggers down a crooked trail and doesn't even
> realize where it leads. So now, my sons, listen to me.
> Never stray from what I am about to say: Run from
> her! Don't go near the door of her house! If you do,
> you will lose your honor and hand over to merciless
> people everything you have achieved in life. Strangers
> will obtain your wealth, and someone else will enjoy
> the fruit of your labor. Afterward you will groan in
> anguish when disease consumes your body, and you

> will say, "How I hated discipline! If only I had not demanded my own way! Oh, why didn't I listen to my teachers? Why didn't I pay attention to those who gave me instruction? I have come to the brink of utter ruin, and now I must face public disgrace." Drink water from your own well—share your love only with your wife. Why spill the water of your springs in public, having sex with just anyone? You should reserve it for yourselves. Don't share it with strangers.
>
> —Proverbs 5:3–17, nlt

The above scripture speaks of diseases. What are some of those diseases? Here are a few common ones: Gonorrhea, Chlamydia, trichomoniasis, genital herpes, genital warts, syphilis, chancroids, and AIDS. And they are rampant. There are strands of sexually transmitted diseases that are being created all the time, and many have no cure. How many people think, "if only I didn't…, if only I hadn't hated instruction." No matter how self-destructive a person is, there probably is not one (sane) person on the planet with an incurable sexually transmitted disease who wishes they had not contracted the disease.

Fornication stops our lives from abounding—being prosperous and growing

As I stated earlier, the Scripture warns us in 1 Thessalonians 4:1, "This is how you should walk so you will abound [increase and be blessed] more and more."

Final word: "For this is the *will of God*, even your sanctification, [path to holiness and cleansing], that you should abstain [don't do it] from fornication" (1 Thess. 4:3, emphasis added).

This is the will of God—don't fornicate. True manhood and womanhood are based on an identity founded in Christ, willing to believe and obey and grow, love and serve. That takes time and effort and perseverance, not a quick fix with real or imaginary beings. Once that alignment has begun to the Word of God and the will of God, there is great hope for wholeness and purpose. After all, who are we as believers anyway? True life is not the pursuit of immediate gratification in any realm. It is a walk of faith, growing to the destiny that God designed in your life. Do we live to please ourselves or God? That is the bottom line.

God loves you: God can forgive, heal, and redeem your life if you have engaged in sexual sin, but forsake these sins and live. Make the decision in advance to walk in the ways of God, not the world, because "If you go against the grain, you get splinters, regardless of which neighborhood you're from…" (Rom. 2:11, THE MESSAGE).

Part III

LESBIAN, GAY, BISEXUAL, TRANSGENDERED/TRANSSEXUAL AND QUEER/QUESTIONING ("LGBT" AND "Q")

God So Loved

I AM GOING TO spend some time on this because this issue is at the forefront of our society and is so foundational to our identity in Christ. When we talk about homosexuality (male and female inclusive here), we are not just talking about sexual activity, but a condition of the soul—the mind, will, and emotions—that precedes behavior and choices. As believers, in all things we need to acknowledge the possibility of God's redemptive power intersecting with behavior, emotional history, desires, gender identity, heredity, and other possible dynamics of homosexuality.

FIRST: GOD LOVES LGBTQ PEOPLE

In fact:

> For God so loved the world, that he gave his only begotten Son, that whosoever believeth in him should not perish, but have everlasting life. For God sent not his Son into the world to condemn the world; but that the world through him might be saved.
>
> —JOHN 3:16–17

Note that the Bible says that God so loved the "world" that He gave His Son as a sacrifice for the sins of the whole world.

I don't think you can get any more loving than being falsely accused and tried, spit upon, whipped and beaten beyond recognition. And then, after being stripped, to be nailed to a cross for another person, to take on their sins, death, sorrow, sickness, infirmities, shame, curses, and eternity in hell, suffering pain, humiliation, and death. After that He was stuffed in a grave—with the authorities really making sure He stayed dead and in that grave by stationing armed soldiers to guard the grave and sealing the stone. God so loved the world. The world includes everyone: people who love God, who might love God; people who don't love God, and never will; people who have never even heard of Him; people who hate Him. He loved us, good, bad, indifferent, up, down, gay, or straight. He loved us to death. He loved us to abundant life. God couldn't have done anything less than to die for us after sin entered the human race to restore us to our divine estate, redeem us from hell and death, and break the power of the enemy over us. God's love is seen in the sacrificial death of His Son. First John 4:9–10 (NLT) says, "God showed how much he loved us by sending his only Son into the world so that we might have eternal life through him. This is real love. It is not that we loved God, but that he loved us and sent his Son as a sacrifice to take away our sins." That is the ultimate definition of love.

I do not approach this topic with condemnation, but with the love and truth of Jesus Christ. Jesus didn't come to condemn; He came to save, to intervene, and replace His life for ours. The Lord Jesus Christ is the Word and definer of "love" and He is the Truth. He invites us to be enraptured with His love, and then He makes us into real people in His image. Jesus treats all people the same; He offers His amazing grace, compelling love, and holy truth to everyone. We can all be changed by His love and truth. It is a process without judgment on our origins, but with correction for our ultimate destiny and destination. That is the gospel. Take away this message and there is no gospel.

Truth. We need to understand that God loving us does

not mean an "anything goes" attitude with God as an excuse, because we are all diverse, and "that's just how I am." God knows we are different physically, historically, emotionally, morally, and spiritually. His goal is oneness with Him and each other through the Cross (John 17). God does have commandments, statutes, paths of life—Jesus Christ is the divine pattern for living—He is the Way, the Truth, and the Life. Paul writes about Christ in us, and "it is no longer I who live," but Christ in me (Gal. 2:20, NLT). And Psalm 16:11 says, "Thou wilt show me the path of life: in thy presence is fullness of joy; at thy right hand there are pleasures for evermore." There truly is a path of life with the Lord.

Love. When we invite Jesus to come into our hearts as Lord and Savior, He absolutely accepts us where we are at that time, and day by day. We can't be righteous or change ourselves anyway. Jesus never said to anyone, "You are just in a category that I can't handle or accept. I am incapable of loving or forgiving you." We may be incapable of loving or forgiving ourselves at times, but He is not incapable of loving or forgiving us. You don't have to be good enough to come to the Savior. Jesus died to save us, not condemn us. He doesn't condemn us for our sins or brokenness; in fact the whole point of the Cross was to place our sins and brokenness on His back, so He could give us His righteousness and wholeness. He takes our death, we take His life. We become like Jesus, because He mercifully became like us, taking all that we are not so we could become all that He is.

More. When we do come to Him, He will work changes in our lives—to separate us from sin, from an old nature that only seeks its own way. We can expect Him to start healing our hearts and lives if we want that, and expect Him to give us a new image and purpose—that is for everyone. When we accept Jesus Christ as Lord and Savior, God is living in us, and God wants to live in a house that embraces and displays His character and destiny for believers—that is for everyone. By the power of His cleansing blood, and the power of the

Holy Spirit, God is actively at work in creating sons and daughters of God in His image, not ours—if we let Him. He is radical, relational, and revolutionary. By His extreme love for and working in us, He changes us. Romans 8:14 says, "For as many as are led by the Spirit of God, they are the sons of God." Through Jesus Christ we again have the possibility of being led of the Spirit of God, rather than the soul and flesh realm.

When He is Lord, we give Him control. If we don't give Him control, we will stay in our sins and brokenness (as the Word of God defines them). That is true for everyone—gay, straight, transgender, transsexual, and everything in between. We cannot expect the miracle working power of God to work in our lives unless and until we place our lives into the miracle working hands of God. If we do yield to Him humbly, day by day, we can expect Him to forgive us of our sins, and undo adaptations to pain or neglect and other emotional conditions and bondages that facilitate sin—going back to conception and generationally. In a profound way, all believers must also accept Him where He is at, too. He intends to recreate us in His image—righteous, holy, loving, obedient, and according to original creative design and the pattern of Jesus Christ. That is His original and His final plan. He is the Alpha and Omega. Follow the pattern. Engage in the process.

Jesus Christ is dangerous—He changes lives. He lays an ax to the root of the trees in our lives through the "tree" of the Cross. In other words, He will lay the ax to all that is not like Him (anger, jealousy, identities and false selves, unforgiveness, rebellion, defenses, and bitterness, as well as damage, pain, and losses, which were inflicted on us, our very selves, our old nature and its fruits and roots), so the likeness of Christ may grow. Once we touch the cross, we expose ourselves to the power of the Holy Spirit, the Word, and the cleansing of the blood—the most powerful forces in the universe.

GAY AND BORN THAT WAY?

First of all, homosexuality as a state of being (being born homosexual) is not recognized in Scripture. Conduct, desires, and emotional conditioning, for example, are the product of many factors and components. No one is born with the same emotional history or natural predisposition, but the Word of God declares that we are all born into a sinful and damaged state and are in need of a Savior. Therefore, when the Lord commands us to love Him with our "hearts," including our mind, will, and emotions, we are commanded to place our hearts under the Lordship of Jesus Christ and the Word of God. God wants to give everyone a "new nature" in the image of His Son—however long it takes, bit by bit, day by day. Follow the pattern; engage in the process. He loves us as we are—that will never change—but part of that love is also to have faith for us, and hope for us, according to His plan for us, like any good parent. Life and growth are part of His plan.

We need to understand that the Lord deals with our sinfulness (thoughts and actions outside of the will of God as revealed in Scripture) and our brokenness (injuries and damage in our emotions and spirits). Jesus died on the cross to do this. His Word is a letter written in His blood. We also need to understand that if an orientation or predisposition is broken down, it consists in part of emotional patterns and responses, memories, and imprints on our souls—some good, some bad. It is also the work of the Cross to dismantle patterns and responses that are ungodly, forgive sins, break curses, expel demons, and heal injuries, restore developmental gaps, and release us from pain, to "renew" and "sanctify" our feelings and responses for all believers.

Jesus Himself said that God created male and female, and that they (male and female) were joined in marriage; gender and sexual expression were defined practically from "day one"—actually day six. I only say this to clarify that God's creative design and order for gender is male and female, and sexual expression is heterosexual. Gender identity and God's designed sexual orientation were established at creation. Gender is very important because it deals with the very image of God, and departure from what God has created challenges the image of God—that's why it is a big deal. God blessed male and female (Gen. 1:27–28). There are two messages here—the blessing of gender and blessing their unity.

Sexual orientation and expression are important because, among other reasons, they deal with God's plan of multiplying the human race and having us exercise dominion in the earth under Him. The oneness, joy, pleasure, and love of the man and woman in marriage reflects Christ and His church.

> Then God said, "Let Us make man in Our image, according to Our likeness; let them have dominion over the fish of the sea, over the birds of the air, and over the cattle, over all the earth and over every creeping thing that creeps on the earth." So God created man in His own image; in the image of God He created him; male and female He created them.
> —Genesis 1:26–27, nkjv

> Therefore a man shall leave his father and mother and be joined to his wife, and they shall become one flesh.
> —Genesis 2:24, nkjv

Homosexual relations, whether physical or emotional, do not affirm God's design beginning with creation including the oneness, holiness, and wholeness He intends.

Born gay? Sexual conduct that the term "homosexual" implies is certainly not the realm of children, babies, fetuses, or embryos. Therefore, the homosexual (emotional) condition or disposition or orientation is the correct focus. Some might say that a person is inclined or predisposed in that direction. But even if that is the case, it is not the equivalent of being "born gay." There is no "gay gene." Biological or genetic factors may contribute to a person's disposition, but there is no inevitability of being gay. As Joseph Nicolosi writes in his excellent book, *Shame and Attachment Loss, The Practical Work of Reparative Therapy*, susceptibility is not inevitability.[1]

Individuals can be more predisposed to homosexuality because of any number of reasons, some environmental and emotional (such as family of origin dynamics and opportunity), and some genetic and biological, such as inherited temperament. But in the end, to engage in homosexual acts is going to be an affirmative choice (not talking about non-consensual sex), no matter how predisposed an individual is, just like any number of other behaviors that have genetic, biological, emotional, and environmental components to them. (I have not even gotten into the spiritual elements of homosexuality yet, such as generational curses and patterns.)

The issue is, of course, that in our society homosexual acts and orientation cannot be considered sin or out of order (what is sin anyway, we're all good?), because people are born that way (unchangeable homosexual condition or predisposition) and have no desire to be another way. While we need to have compassion on the origins of behavior, we also need to respond with truth on God's intent and power to transform—the Cross or the world. However a person feels they are born does not negate God's design and His redemptive power, or negate the fact that we are all sinners one way or another. Obviously, Father God thought the whole world was facing a serious eternal crisis, and so He sent His Son Jesus to save us (everyone) through an excruciating death on the cross, from eternal condemnation because of our sins—thoughts and actions out of the will of God. As stated earlier, we are blessed when the Lord identifies "sin" as "sin." The Scripture has defined a clear position on homosexuality.

Perhaps moving to homosexual relations, whether physical or emotional, may be very "natural" to some, and abstaining from homosexual relations would be a struggle or considered even unnecessary. But the Bible position has to be reckoned with, with regard to gender identity, emotions, lifestyle, and sexual relations. We must submit to God's position that we are all born sinners and all born broken, so sin and brokenness is "natural" to natural born sinners. This is true even if there is no knowledge of truth in this area, or desire to agree with the truth of the Word of God, or there exists a predisposition—like any number of behaviors, attitudes, or emotional conditions. We are all "hard-wired" to sin. We are all broken for many reasons. Remember Jesus came to heal the brokenhearted and set the captives free (Luke 4:18). Romans 5:12 (NLT) says, "When Adam sinned, sin entered the entire human race. Adam's sin brought death, so death spread to everyone, for everyone sinned." That was for everybody.

Similarly, generations may be predisposed to alcohol or drug abuse for environmental, biological, genetic, and emotional reasons as well as spiritual reasons, but eventually someone has to lift a glass to their mouth, or take a hit. These practices may change the physical or mental state of the user over time, but at one point, there was choice involved. We as believers can ask for the intervention of the blood of Jesus and the Holy Spirit to restore godly choice and dismantle those emotional and even physical changes that trigger sinful choices.

Further, I believe that the issue of generational curses moves in part in this way: When we experience emotional damage due to our own sin, or we are sinned against, or the opportunity simply presents itself, the generational curse leads us to a sinful generational pattern which is part of the sin nature, to act out brokenness. Perhaps some people are drawn to the occult, and some to greed, and others to homosexuality. I have heard people say, I was just so attracted to the occult. Why is that? Probably because generational sins opened the door for their choice. You may hate something, through no goodness of your own, that deeply attracts another person and vice versa. Despite the ease or inevitability in which a person falls into *any* sin or pattern of living, or the "non-choice" nature of the choice, it is still a reflection of the sinful and broken condition that the Lord wants to forgive and root up so that we may be saved, healed, and restored.

In our world, however, gay has become an identity and lifestyle with its own theology, history, legal status, emotional justification, and other validations that harden the position of those who self-identify as gay. This is a deeper issue, a lifestyle issue based on an orientation, the argument goes. Yes, it is difficult to back out of an identity—any identity—because identities comprise our emotional, social, sexual, and physical life; but in the end, we all must back out of our old identities, and take on a new identity in Christ with His character and holiness. A deep emotional condition related to the gay lifestyle does not have its own "sacredness" any more than "self" has its own sacredness. It is still subject to God and can be transformed by the power of the Cross, the power of the Resurrection, the power of the Word of God, and the power of the Holy Spirit.

Consider the identity that Paul the Apostle had:

> Yet I could have confidence in myself if anyone could. If others have reason for confidence in their own efforts, I have even more! For I was circumcised when I was eight days old, having been born into a pure-blooded Jewish family that is a branch of the tribe of Benjamin. So I am a real Jew if there ever was one! What's more, I was a member of the Pharisees, who demand the strictest obedience to the Jewish law. And zealous? Yes, in fact, I harshly persecuted the church. And I obeyed the Jewish law so carefully that I was never accused of any fault. I once thought all these things were so very important, but now I consider them worthless because of what Christ has done. Yes, everything else is worthless when compared with the priceless gain of knowing Christ Jesus my Lord. I have discarded everything else, counting it all as garbage, so that I may have Christ and become one with him. I no longer count on my own goodness or my ability

to obey God's law, but I trust Christ to save me. For God's way of making us right with himself depends on faith. As a result, I can really know Christ and experience the mighty power that raised him from the dead. I can learn what it means to suffer with him, sharing in his death, so that, somehow, I can experience the resurrection from the dead!

— PHILIPPIANS 3:4–11, NLT

The apostle Paul was as elite as anyone could be in his society. He was a circumcised pure-blooded Jew, establishing his own righteousness by the law, a Pharisee, and a persecutor of the church. He had an elevated place in society, and a generational identity—the ultimate identity. But in the end, all of that was worthless compared to the priceless gain of knowing Christ. In the end it is about knowing Christ, the power of His resurrection and the fellowship of His sufferings (Phil. 3:10).

In short, the question is, What leads peoples to their choices? And here is the deeper realm we must explore. Here is what we can say about everyone—gay, straight, outside, and in between.

Sin and the Sin Nature

Everyone sins and everyone is born a sinner. Jesus came to forgive sins (the fruit of our sin nature)—though that is only one level. In a deeper level, the Cross puts an ax to our sin nature. The sin nature is replaced with a new nature through the new birth in Christ by the seed of the Word, watered by the Holy Spirit growing us into new creations. Additionally, we die daily, as Paul says, as we walk in obedience. That is called dying to self. The ax cuts deeper and Christ grows stronger, day by day. As far as homosexual behavior and fantasies are concerned, Jesus took these on Himself at the Cross, just like all sin of people who consider themselves heterosexual, and any other sin or iniquity (perverse moral bent) of the human race, originating from whomever, whether in the heart or acted out. The issue here is accepting the truth of the Word of God or not (marriage and gender as described in Scripture is the pattern for sexual relations for all the reasons we have described). If not, then that is a choice. If so, then that is a decision as well. But in the Word of God nobody is defined by his or her sexual orientation or homosexual condition before God. Have you seen that anywhere in the Bible?

Perhaps the traditional Christian approach to homosexuality was to just encourage the person (assuming a believer) to repent of homosexual acts, and instruct the believer to refrain from certain behavior. Unfortunately, that does not resolve deeper emotional conflicts and spiritual influences, and does not lead to an affirmative joyful Christian life. Some writers have differentiated between homosexual acts and the homosexual condition. (See Elizabeth Moberly, *Homosexuality a New Christian Ethic*,[2] a very fine book.) It is right to repent of sins—including homosexual acts and fantasies—and it is right to refrain from sinful behavior, and it is right to die daily; but that is only a start for the work of the grace of God in the human heart—the absolute, gentle, compassionate love of God that leads to transformation and holiness, so that we may live with peace out of the center of our lives. My sense is that all sin and desires are a roadmap pointing to the broken places in the soul. God's heart is not for His children simply to live a life of suppression, but expression and expansion in Him, as personal histories are unraveled, and lives healed and restored.

But to receive what God has for us we have to release our lives. That is why Jesus said, "Repent: for the kingdom of heaven is at hand" (Matt. 4:17). We are not going to transition into a new kingdom unless we accept God's perspective and judgment of an old kingdom. We cannot move to the newness of the kingdom by keeping control over our lives and defending ourselves before God—something has to give. Do we want it our way or God's way? In, out, up, or down?

This is not a cut and dried issue or only a sin issue—just like anything else, alcoholism, theft, anger, jealousy, adultery or covetousness, is only a sin issue. The Bible also tends to speak about "acts." Consistent practice gains a label in Scripture, such as "adulterer" or "righteous." Biblically, sinners may have been categorized as "homosexuals" based on sinful practices, but this is not a final category of existence or being, any more than "adulterers" are a final category of existence. The early biblical references to homosexuality are part of the early biblical references to incest and adultery. God does not have a special set of rules regarding the sin, condition, or orientation that leads to homosexual acts and relations, and orientation to sin and brokenness that lead to any other sinful acts or may be acted out by someone not identified as homosexual. That's an important point, since there is no "special treatment" on the road to the Cross. He desires to change all false identities based on sin and the sin nature through His love at the Cross. As the Lordship of Jesus Christ and the power of the Holy Spirit take over more and more of a person's identity and personality, less and less sin becomes "inevitable" for all people.

Also, the desire to do such acts, or anything else that is the fruit of a nature fallen in sin and brokenness (see Galatians 5:19–21), can be reinforced by demonic spirits that pass through the generations or enter through personal experience—like all other sin. In the end this is an issue of walking in the flesh, and just affirming a nature rooted in the flesh (including here by definition a way of thinking and living, hence the term, "carnally minded") or walking in the Spirit ("spiritually minded"). In the case of the homosexual lifestyle, a carnally minded person has developed emotional patterns and relations, and sexual behavior that are simply, well, carnal. I am not trying to negate true friendship or the benefits of any relationship where it exists—that is not the issue. Further, although human love may be true and deep, ultimately the issue is whether the relational pattern glorifies God and is in agreement with His Word—which it does not. But the Bible intends that all believers engage in the process of dismantling the old nature (the Cross), and living out a new nature (the Resurrection) empowered by the Holy Spirit and directed by the Word of God. The fruit stops when the root is cut. This view may seem foolish, unnecessary, and wrong to the carnal, worldly mind. It demonstrates the ancient clash between the world's system and ways of thinking, and the kingdom of God. The preaching of the Cross is foolishness to the world, Paul writes (1 Cor. 1:18).

> We preach Christ crucified…Because the foolishness of God is wiser than men; and the weakness of God is stronger than men.
>
> —1 Corinthians 1:23, 25

Generational Curses

There may be generational curses in the area of sexual brokenness that leads to a predisposition to homosexual desires and behavior. As I stated, the generational curse is a channel whereby people act out brokenness and desires in a particular sinful pattern, and there are demonic influences that can reinforce this. There can be a predisposition (automatic built-in desire) for a type of sin because of generational curses. "…for I the Lord they God am a jealous God, visiting the iniquity [sins and moral illness] of the fathers upon the children unto the third and fourth generation of them that hate me" (Exod. 20:5).

The Lord states at the beginning of the Ten Commandments that sin can be passed on from generation to generation. By the way, blessings can be passed on also. What are some examples of sins and patterns of behavior passed on from generation to generation that we see all the time? Here is a short list: Alcoholism and other addictions, abuse, fornication, and yes, homosexuality. All kinds of other things too—control, religious spirits, pride, occult power, bitterness, and fear.

Whether we like it or not, sin opens the doors for other generations down the line to be damaged and actually defiled with the same problems—it is the law of the seed. But the Lord is also clear with His solution.

Emotional Conditions

Importantly, there are deep emotional conditions that the Holy Spirit must reach. As many have written, a child may experience detachment from a same sex parent that leads to other results—detachment, disidentification, and dissociation from self and even gender, or disruption in the development of gender identity and formation of self. This is why same sex attraction can be so deep, because it may involve early childhood developmental issues and attachment issues, and such persons feel that they are "born gay" based on early sense of a gap, identity question, or need. There are some great sources about these issues that can explain the emotional dynamics of same sex attraction in depth, from a professional perspective. I recommend: Joseph Nicolosi's, *Shame and Attachment Loss, The Practical Work of Reparative Therapy*, which deals with male homosexuality, and Janelle Hallman's, *The Heart of Female Same Sex Attraction*, which deals with female homosexuality. There are also professional websites such as www.narth.com for the National Association for Research & Therapy of Homosexuality.

Some themes: Detachment can be the result of very subtle emotional experiences between parent and child, and flight from pain and shame. This emotional detachment also short-circuits love that child might receive from the same sex parent. Detachment and dissociation from self and gender cause a lifelong search for that home and emotional core that was never built into the person. Disruption in the development of gender identity and self creates a gap that cannot be dismissed. People don't need to be sexually abused or experience massive trauma to start in the path to homosexuality, though sexual abuse certainly can create and increase brokenness and create a barrier to growth until resolved. A child may only be neglected, or experience trauma that adults would consider minor, to begin adaptive changes and behaviors that lead to homosexuality or a homosexual condition. Spiritually, the effect of detachment is living out of a false self as opposed to a true God-designed, God-ordained identity. The real person, the real path of growth has been abandoned for something that will get a measure of attention and protection. God asks, Do we desire the real person or want to live out of a false self forever? This is for all people.

Attachment issues and need for growth are the source of many broken and sinful behaviors, not just homosexuality. Aren't we all looking for love, belonging, and attention? In fact, we all experience attachment loss, because, as born sinners, we do not have intimate relationship with our Father in heaven, the comfort of the Holy Spirit, and the life of Jesus Christ in us. As believers, we need to address losses in God's way. With regard to homosexuality, the Lord intends for brokenness and pain to be processed in a godly way for resolution and not comforted through homosexual encounters and relationships, drugs, or any other "comforter."

Many people experience lack of nurture, lack of affirmation in gender identity, disruption of identity, mal-attunement by the same-sex parent, pain, neglect, and lack of maturation, which can cause a predisposition to certain behavior. The next step would be "fixing" oneself by seeking that missing piece in another person of the same sex, or finding oneself in another. Heterosexuals do that same thing. Individuals can experience gender insecurity or inferiority or disruption at an early age, a feeling of being in a different emotional landscape than their peers. They can detach from their gender and personhood. Nobody is committing actual homosexual acts at this point, but clearly there is a void that has to be filled.

All of the emotional conditions I have mentioned may be related to perfectly legitimate needs that must be filled, or areas that need healing and deliverance. Pain, damage, and need are not about sin; they are about loss and brokenness. How people respond, judge, and adapt, however, can be sinful.

So, how a person fills these gaps or heals these injuries is the issue. Is it through healing, deliverance, growth and formation of a new life by faith through the power of the Holy

Spirit, or a sexual and emotional lifestyle in opposition to God's Word? Is it through fellowship with believers in godly relationships, godly help and counsel, and fellowship with the Holy Spirit, or fellowship with the world? Simply, people try to repair themselves. It is only when we are born again that we can look backwards and grow up again forward in the nature and nurture of Jesus Christ. With regard to homosexuality, I know this is not politically correct. There is a strong lobby in this country that says sexual destiny is fixed (except when someone who was heterosexual moves to homosexuality), but that is not so according to the Word of God. The Lord creates a new destiny and if we enter into His destiny, He has great promises and life on the other end.

The church of Jesus Christ is here to encourage and help people through love, and speaking the truth in love, to enter into relationship with Jesus Christ and find themselves in Christ. This is what we do at our church because we are all equal in the sight of God. We encourage believers to step into the stream of Christ's love for them, and then learn and grow. Jesus asked the man at the pool of Bethesda if he wanted to be made whole. The man had been there a long time. Jesus must have thought the question was important. But at Jesus's command, the man walked. There must be a willingness to be healed and made whole, even if feelings seem to be going an opposite direction. (Notice in the story of the man at the pool of Bethesda that no one else clamored for healing from Jesus after the man took his mat and walked away. What does that tell you?) And here is how we receive from the Lord: "Every morning you'll hear me at it again. Every morning I lay out the pieces of my life on your altar and watch for fire to descend" (Ps. 5:3, THE MESSAGE). Surrender, submission, faith, experiencing grief; all these are ways God can work.

In the end, many people who are pursuing the gay life-style are attempting to resolve early childhood or generational issues, to repair themselves because of an emptiness and loss that can't even be defined. Some writers have called this a "reparative" drive. It is deep and compelling. The romantic, emotional, or sexual pursuit becomes a pursuit for a connected self, source of affirmation and growth, and identity. This search is very compelling because it involves developmental issues and damage for the most part that must be addressed. However, homosexual behavior doesn't really fix or repair the roots of the drive, but essentially covers up the conflicts, pain, shame, trauma, emotional damage, and gaps in growth. These are the true issues, not the homosexuality. The resultant homosexual behavior and its rewards actually make it harder for true restoration.

All of this may be emotionally experienced at a young age. Consequently, the person believes they are "born gay" when they are older and sexual expression or strong emotional attachments outside of family begin. Somehow such predisposed children did not share the same emotional world as others of their gender, feeling "different" because they never had the same sense of gender, gender roles, attachment, formation of self, and general socialization patterns that other children experienced. This does not preclude such conflicts being awakened later in life either. All children need role models and supportive adults that affirm their true identity and help them to grow to maturity. When this does not happen or there are weak, abusive, neglectful, absent parents, or caregivers, parents with their own deep problems and unmet needs, the child is "on his own" to figure out life and identity. (Another note, feeling "different" doesn't mean a person is gay; maybe God has a peculiar plan for their lives.)

In short, many people say that they were attracted to the same sex when they were very young. But these feelings didn't just happen. Further, they may feel that way, but that doesn't mean that God designed those desires in their hearts or that it is His intended plan. Just because a person has an emotional or physical desire, no matter how strong, doesn't mean it is from God.

Every believer must answer these questions: Will I will live out my life as I feel, or will I look to who He is and being conformed to His image? Will we live God-centered lives as opposed to self-centered lives? Only the Holy Spirit and the Word of God, and a yielded vessel, can truly bring restraint in the boundaries our lives, and creatively move individuals into God's patterns for living. The Holy Spirit and the Word of God liberate our choices for righteousness. That doesn't mean believers will make godly choices every time or that longtime emotional patterns or physical responses are quickly resolved and overcome; it just means believers now have the spiritual tools to move as the Lord desires. The deep renewing of the mind, meaning our mental and emotional condition, enables us to live out new patterns for being a living sacrifice (Rom. 12:1–2). Sacrifice, interesting word—perhaps we can say, it is not fun every minute, but worth it in Christ.

No one can claim before God, "This is just how I am wired," if our desires and behavior and emotional condition do not line up with Scripture. God, the same God that created the earth and raised Jesus from the dead, is willing and able to do a work of resurrection and restoration in that spirit, soul, and body. When the Holy Spirit begins to do a work in each heart, its fruits will progressively be in line with the nature of Jesus Christ and the Word of God. All of Christian living is process of relearning, renewing, restoration, sanctification, obedience, healing, and struggle. But the fruits of righteousness are well worth any struggle. Gay or straight isn't a final category—it is an artificial differentiation. All must be transformed into His image, and it is a process. It is the walk of the Cross. The entire human race is born into brokenness and sin, but the existence of the Cross of Jesus Christ declares the potential of a new life to those who believe in the fullness of that life and want to work out their salvation with fear and trembling.

Change is a process. Nothing is instantaneous in the kingdom of heaven with regard to what Christians would call "sanctification," or being made holy, "righteousness," right living in relationship with the Lord, His people, and commands, and "whole" living with soundness of mind, emotions, body, and spirit. But the Lord calls all His people to travel this journey. John 1:12 says, "But as many as received him, to them gave he power to *become* the sons of God, even to them that believe on his name" (emphasis added). We now have the power to become sons of God. *This is very important*: "Becoming" is a process, a journey with the Lord, enabled by an internal power from God. It doesn't mean you will never be tempted in an area, or avoid struggle, or suddenly arrive with new desires. It means that you have submitted yourself to being transformed into the image of Christ by the love and truth of Christ and the power of the Holy Spirit. All believers are called to be in the process of allowing God to define and direct their lives, desires, imaginations, emotions, goals, and identity day by day. We are called to holiness.

> Behold what manner of love the Father has bestowed on us, that we should be called children of God! Therefore the world does not know us, because it did not know Him. Beloved, now we are children of God; and it has not yet been revealed what we shall be, but we know that when He is revealed, we shall be like Him, for we shall see Him as He is. And everyone who has this hope in Him purifies himself, just as He is pure.
>
> —1 John 3:1–3, nkjv

We are the children of God. We don't know exactly what we will be, but have the hope that when He is revealed we will be like Him. If we have this hope then we purify ourselves.

In my view, the roots of same sex attraction are not happy, nurturing events, but failures, traumas, grief, disappointments, shame, neglect, mal-attunement, need for growth and development, and heartaches that need to be dealt with by the forgiveness of the Cross and the power of the Holy Spirit. Many homosexuals say that no one would choose to be born gay. Perhaps this is a clue that such desires and emotional disposition are not "gifts" from God, because gifts from God bring life and joy. James 1:17 (NLT) says, "Whatever is good and perfect comes to us from God above, who created all heaven's lights. Unlike them, he never changes or casts shifting shadows." Proverbs 10:22 (NLT) says, "The blessing of the Lord makes a person rich, and he adds no sorrow with it." There is no sorrow when God gives a gift.

So if a person feels they are "gay," "different," "queer," or "questioning," it is valuable to get to the bottom of these "feelings." Some relevant questions are: How much did you bond with your same sex parent? Were they there for you, did they hear you? Did they affirm your gender—or life at all? Did they show you how to behave and grow in a healthy way? Did they impart a positive or any sense of your gender to you? Were they whole people? Was there a real and validating connection? Perhaps there was a death in the family or physical distance—how did this affect you? Were you angry with them and want to distance yourself from the image of femininity or masculinity that you saw in them, or were they admirable role models? Was it safe, rewarding, or fun to be female or male, or even yourself with your gifts, growing up in your home? Were you injured, rejected, or hurt deeply in other ways? In short, did you like what you saw, who you were, and what you got?

The Good News is in Luke 4:18–19. Jesus said:

> The Spirit of the Lord is upon me, because he hath anointed me to preach the gospel to the poor; he hath sent me to heal the brokenhearted, to preach deliverance to the captives, and recovering of sight to the blind, to set at liberty them that are bruised, To preach the acceptable year of the Lord.

Jesus is the healer of broken hearts. He is the grower of souls. He is the renewer of our minds. The Bible says that Jesus saves to the "uttermost." In other words, there is not a sin, condition, thought, or behavior that cannot be redeemed and transformed by Jesus. He is the *extreme Savior* of the *world*. Making a political cause out of a condition does not change the Word of God or the love of the Savior.

Just some final words, we live in an environment that promotes sexual curiosity and experimentation. This is particularly true today in the "bi-curious" world of young people who are encouraged to explore all sexual feelings, fantasies, and connections without boundaries. However, people must realize that emotional patterns are being set and hardened, even with experimentation.

There are unclean, familiar, and perverse spirits that operate in the sexual realm, and these spirits also can be passed to an individual through the generations or personal sinful activities. These spirits enhance sinful behavior. I am not saying that everything is "demonic" but there can be spiritual forces involved in desires and behavior. Therefore, to "feel" gay doesn't mean, in the bigger picture, that the feelings being experienced originate from God; or with regard to immediate feelings, that the temptations are internal. If we went by our "feelings," everything on the planet would be permissible, and it would be in complete meltdown (though we are almost there).

Many issues in our lives have several levels—the sin level, generational curses, demonic, emotional brokenness and pain, lack of growth, environmental influence, family dynamics and others. Jesus came to meet the needs of the total person and bring total wholeness.

As with all behavior and attitudes, if our desires or actions do not line up with the Word of God, then we repent and seek God's help. That does not mean that the Lord does not love you because His Word describes sinful or broken behavior and conditions. He loves you deeply and wants to bring you through a process to a promise, and that is wholeness and holiness in Him, and all the blessings He has for you. He also corrects and disciplines His children. Hebrews 12:5–6 (NLT) says, "And have you entirely forgotten the encouraging words God spoke to you, his children? He said, 'My child, don't ignore it when the Lord disciplines you, and don't be discouraged when he corrects you. For the Lord disciplines those he loves, and he punishes those he accepts as his children.'" God's correction of us is proof of His love and fatherhood.

Some More Scriptures

Remember what Jesus says about fornication—this includes homosexual behavior:

> For from within, out of the heart of men, proceed evil thoughts, adulteries, fornications, murders, thefts... all these evil things come from within, and defile the man.
>
> —Mark 7:21–23

Jesus identifies all sexual sin as sin, of any variety, including homosexual fornication. A lot of people say that Jesus did not talk about homosexual acts. He did. He called it "fornication," and that covers everything. If a person has sex outside of the covenant of marriage as set up by the Word of God as early as the Book of Genesis, is it not fornication even if it is between two persons of the same gender? If a man has sex outside of marriage with a woman, it is adultery. But if it is with a man, is it something different than adultery? The very fact that Jesus does not differentiate between heterosexual and homosexual acts outside of marriage is a message in itself. There is no special category for homosexual activities. Notice before Jesus talks about these activities, He prefaces His commentary with "evil thoughts," so that the imagination precedes the action and is considered "evil" in itself.

The modern revision is that being gay or lesbian is immutable (it can't be changed) or it is an inborn condition. Therefore, homosexual acts are excused from the category of "fornication" and that orientation or preference or desire or identity or free expression cannot be changed. In fact, the Bible is out of date, or must be revised to the modern understanding of this issue. Or there is no biblical standard, because homosexuality exists, and everything else must adjust, including God. But God is God—because He is, and has the last and final word. He is the Lord and He changes not. God and His Word are one. He is Creator of heaven and earth, and Redeemer of mankind. He provides a process of forgiveness, healing, and deliverance to set captives free through His beloved Son.

The Scripture also refers to "Those who indulge in sexual sin, who are idol worshipers, adulterers, male prostitutes, homosexuals, thieves, greedy people, drunkards, abusers, and swindlers—none of these will have a share in the Kingdom of God. There was a time when some of you were just like that, but now your sins have been washed away [*forgiveness and cleansing*], and you have been set apart for God [*holiness and the work of the Holy Spirit*]. You have been made right with God [*soundness of heart and mind and right standing with God*] because of what the Lord Jesus Christ and the Spirit of our God have done for you. (See 1 Corinthians 6:9–11, NLT.) The King James Version of the Bible says it this way in verse 11: "Such were some of you"—so this is not an unchangeable condition when the power of the Cross and the Resurrection are applied.

Paul is clear about transformation. Second Corinthians 5:17 (NKJV) says: "Therefore, if anyone is in Christ, he is a new creation; old things have passed away; behold, all things have become new." The Amplified Bible states: "Therefore if any person is [ingrafted] in Christ (the Messiah) he is a new creation (a new creature altogether); the old [previous moral and spiritual condition] has passed away. Behold, the fresh and new has come!" The church of Jesus Christ is commissioned to open the door to everyone, and create an environment by ministering love and truth, so the Holy Spirit can do His work in hearts to create new men and women.

It is a lie of the enemy that a sinful, broken condition or person in need of maturation and healing cannot be changed or need not be changed (like all people born on the planet). Then why did Christ die? Why do we have the Holy Spirit? If He just wanted to pat us on the back and affirm us as to where we are, in our sinfulness and brokenness, He could have stayed in heaven and skipped the agony. "That's OK, do what you want, I'm all love, so anything goes." Rather, He is the "Lamb of God who takes away the sin of the world" (John 1:29). He died in agony and shame that we may live a new life. A relationship with God is not about "self-realization," but "God realization," and God realization puts Him and His Word first, in the center of our lives—not self-worship or all the voices we hear around us.

God sent His Son to create a new nature and new identity in us, one designed in heaven—one borne in the image of His Son. He wants to strip away that which is false—an identity established in sin and brokenness, the will of the flesh, this world, and the devil—and give us a new nature rooted and grounded in His love. To assume or declare that a person is born gay or transgendered, for example, or any other definition out there, and must stay that way, is an identity theft of massive proportions. It keeps such persons or limits them from the power, purposes, pleasure, position, personality, and passion that God designed for them from the foundation of the world, and is contrary to Scripture.

The good news is that God's original design is a divine pattern in everyone, and like all experiences in the kingdom, by the guidance of the Holy Spirit and the Word of God, that original design can be rediscovered. There is *not* a void. There is something to go backwards to—original creative design— and something to go forward to—Jesus Christ in us.

Another scripture is in Romans chapter 1; Paul describes those who depart from the truth of God, one result being homosexuality. Romans 1:31 also talks about being "without natural affection." Here are some aspects of this concept: Outside of the boundaries of God's design, order, and love, or not having affection where it should be placed. There is also "natural affection," which is according to God's design and order. Finally there is "supernatural affection," which is the agape love of God, which expresses the love of God through ordinary people in a holy way. Just as an aside, a lot of people (in sexual relationships), gay or straight, love each other and exhibit deep sacrifice, compassion, and commitment outside of the marriage covenant described in Scripture. Nevertheless, such relationships still do not follow the commands of God or glorify God. In the end if we love Him, we will obey His commandments (John 14:15). The most loving thing on the planet we can do is to lead someone to Jesus and the ways of God.

Scriptures in Leviticus 18:22 and 20:13 prohibit homosexuality. For most sexual sin under the old covenant brought to God's people by Moses the punishment was death—not just homosexuality, but adultery and fornication were included. We now live under a covenant of grace. Jesus has taken our punishment if we receive His forgiveness. While the penalty for sin shifted under the new covenant, God's moral law never changed. Jesus came to fulfill the law. Moral laws concerning adultery and homosexuality, for example, are not the equivalent of the dietary laws, one step away from eating shellfish, which is not relevant under the new covenant, except with regard to food offered to idols, or the ceremonial law, the ordinances, sacrifices and feasts that are done away and fulfilled in Christ. But the New Testament still covers many types of sexual sin, including homosexuality. *All* sin leads to spiritual death:

> For the wages of sin is death; but the gift of God is eternal life through Jesus Christ our Lord.
>
> —ROMANS 6:23

> There is a way which seemeth right unto a man, but the end thereof are the ways of death.
>
> —PROVERBS 14:12

God's Solution

Jesus has a big solution for everyone who says that they were born gay, lesbian, bisexual or transgender, and any other sexual identity. In John 3:3, Jesus says: "Except a man be *born again,* he cannot see the kingdom of heaven." This goes for everybody. We all come from the same direction to the Cross—there are no special categories. The old nature that is corrupt and predisposed to sin must die, and a new nature based in Jesus Christ is born in us by the power of the Holy Spirit. This is called the "new birth." The fruit of the old nature is sin, but the fruit of the new nature is righteousness. The new birth reaches back to our very beginnings. So, instead of trying to fulfill God's leading and commands with a sin nature—which is impossible—believers in Jesus Christ have a new nature from God, a nature that desires to do the will of God. We do this by His grace. We stand by His grace (Rom. 5:2). We abound in His grace (2 Cor. 9:8). We are strong in His grace (2 Tim. 2:1). We grow in His grace (2 Pet. 3:18). Paul said, "I am who I am through the grace of God" (1 Cor. 15:10). Also be filled with the Holy Spirit, which is a source of power and testimony to others (Acts 1:8).

Another major part of God's solution for addressing this habitual sin is to seek forgiveness for participation in homosexual acts; break soul ties and ungodly covenants with homosexual lovers; forgive, as applicable, parents who may have been absent, rejecting, neglectful, controlling and abusive; forgive, if applicable, those who may have sexually abused you; seek release in areas where you may have been traumatized, including accidents, sickness, disability, betrayal, sexual abuse, neglect, or rejection; process the grief, pain, and brokenness in your life, and ask the Lord to fill the gaps created by this destructive behavior. Get some help from pastors, therapists, and counselors who have ministered in this area. Be accountable to other mature Christians. It often takes the counsel, prayers, and assistance of others to help unravel life.

Guided prayers can speed the process. The Holy Spirit cuts across time.

In this unpacking process, layers and layers of grief, pain, and sin are released and cleansed. Usually there is deep-rooted shame that must be dealt with, false identities and selves used for protection and to mediate life that need to be released instead of embraced. Processing and release from these elements and very real losses are an important part of healing. The Holy Spirit is there to help you. It is important to assign blame where it is due, and then forgive, rather than carry personal shame.

Finally, if there is a need for growth where love stopped, perhaps it is a jump from three to four years old, then five to six and so on, the Holy Spirit can enable this. All of this can take a while, and may be happening simultaneously. God can fill in the gaps that were missing. David prayed, create in me a new and clean heart and renew a right spirit (Ps. 51:10). God can creatively work to build hearts. He can restore the years the locust and cankerworm have eaten away (Joel 2:25). And He can revive His people in the midst of years (Hab. 3:2).

A person also needs to break generational patterns of fornication and homosexuality in his or her life. It is valuable for mature believers to minister healing to a person's heart, dealing with spiritual elements such as forgiveness and repentance, generational patterns/curses, souls ties, and demonic influences, as well as ministering the healing in areas of pain and shame, and releasing the Holy Spirit to restart true growth. This is a layer-by-layer process that may take a while, but has great power and great value. I like the words of Psalm 32:1–5 in the Amplified Bible:

> BLESSED (HAPPY, fortunate, to be envied) is he who has forgiveness of his transgression continually exercised upon him, whose sin is covered. Blessed (happy, fortunate, to be envied) is the man to whom the Lord imputes no iniquity and in whose spirit there

> is no deceit. When I kept silence [before I confessed],
> my bones wasted away through my groaning all the
> day long. For day and night Your hand [of displeasure]
> was heavy upon me; my moisture was turned into the
> drought of summer. Selah [pause, and calmly think of
> that]! I acknowledged my sin to You, and my iniquity
> I did not hide. I said, I will confess my transgressions
> to the Lord [continually unfolding the past till all is
> told]—then You [instantly] forgave me the guilt and
> iniquity of my sin. Selah [pause, and calmly think of
> that]!

The psalmist was "continually unfolding the past until all
is told." While I believe that such unfolding is important for
the forgiveness of sins, mixed in the process are all the losses,
damage, fears, hurt, and abuses of others that have fueled the
sins. Tell the story; let it unfold.

Finally, Jesus calls us to go to the cross and die to the flesh.
This is the path of the believer, not self-indulgence. Jesus says,
"If any man will come after Me, let him deny himself, and
take up his cross, and follow Me" (Matt. 16:24). God calls all
believers to a lifetime walk of obedience. He promises a life of
real joy. The Holy Spirit can deliver, restore, and rebuild lives.
That is the power of the Cross and the Resurrection. This is
not just for those who have same sex attraction.

One final thought on this: God wants to give us all (gay or
straight) a new identity so that we can have a divine destiny
in Him. If you consider yourself gay, you cannot cling to that
identity or that lifestyle any more than any "straight" person
is permitted to cling to any identity outside of the will of God.
God is in the business of changing all of us into the image of
His Son, who was without sin. The hardest thing for all people
to give up is control of their lives, and the identity to which
they are emotionally attached. But that identity may well be
the "strong man" that keeps out the power of God in your life
and the true destiny that God has for you.

What is Jesus like? The writer of Hebrews says He is "holy, harmless, and undefiled" (Heb. 7:26). He is our pattern for living. He is holy, that is His nature, because He is God—the Bible tells us to "be ye holy, for I am holy." He is harmless, He did not disobey the Word of God when He walked on earth, and He walked in love. He never added to the pain or burdens of others. Rather He lifted burdens—He was the servant of the world. He was undefiled. He did not enter into any sin in thought or deed that defiled His nature. What is pure religion? James 1:27 says, "Pure religion and undefiled before God and the Father is this, To visit the fatherless and widows in their affliction, and to keep himself unspotted from the world." It is a compassionate and holy walk. We are to be like Him.

There's a pattern here to remember in the Bible—*death and resurrection, death and resurrection, death and resurrection*—die to self, live to God, and there will be much fulfillment and fruitfulness. Even Jesus had to die to come to His destiny from the foundation of the world. He tells us all in John 12:24–26 (NKJV): "Most assuredly, I say to you, unless a grain of wheat falls into the ground and dies, it remains alone; but if it dies, it produces much grain. He who loves his life will lose it, and he who hates his life in this world will keep it for eternal life. If anyone serves Me, let him follow Me; and where I am, there My servant will be also. If anyone serves Me, him My Father will honor." Dying is part of the process of abundant life and fruitfulness. To the rest, Mark 8:36 (NKJV): "For what will it profit a man if he gains the whole world, and loses his own soul?" *Death and resurrection, death and resurrection, death and resurrection*…just remember that. But the results are worth it, as seen in this scripture:

O taste and see that the LORD is good.

—PSALM 34:8

Bisexuality

The bisexual is attracted sexually to members of both sexes. The bisexual person is still subject to the scriptural position on marriage and fornication. Similarly, a man can claim attraction to two women—his wife and another woman. That does not justify adultery.

A Note on Jesus and Gender

Gender identity and sexual orientation in the world's definitions may be viewed as some form of continuum where an individual may fall anywhere on the scale from a masculine, heterosexual male, for example, to transsexual, male to female, or blended sexual identities, and everything in between. This also assumes that the non-biblical models of masculine and feminine identity and behavior, and the world's many definitions of sexuality and gender, are accurate and final. But God doesn't have continuums. God has truth. Male and female created He them—the gender identity He has provided, with sexuality expressed in heterosexual marriage.

God allows plenty of room for different gifts and desires that are not sinful. A sensitive, artistic man is as male as a football player. One of the greatest men of the Bible, David, was a poet and a warrior. Perhaps that was on purpose, as God could show the range of gifts through a man that took authority over a kingdom and killed a giant, but also sang to himself, took care of sheep, played a harp, and invented musical instruments for worship. Jesus had the sensitivity to weep, but also expressed anger at the Pharisees. Deborah, the judge, led a nation. She was a woman chosen for this position by God to liberate Israel, but she was also a wife, and most likely a mother. Deborah was a leader in an important battle; David played a harp.

Here is the obliterator of continuums—each one of us is a unique expression that God designed to be in His image. What is truly masculine and what is truly feminine is seen in a very good example: Jesus Christ. He is righteous, kind, holy, pure, creative, sensitive, tender, loving, nurturing, and expressive, as well as strong, direct, faithful, active, and assertive. Jesus both transcends gender and defines gender and behavior. With regard to behavior, when our behavior conforms to His love and truth, when we love the Lord our God with all our heart, mind, strength, and our neighbor as ourselves, then we will be living out the life of Christ in us, in either a female or male body, gloriously created by the Father, Son, and Holy Spirit. Furthermore, Jesus did not commit sexual sin—it was a question of holiness. We are the temple of the Living God.

Jesus both defines marriage and transcends it. He defines marriage on an earthly realm, but it has a heavenly source and model, and we are all married to Him. All covenantal relationships are combined in Him.

Transgender/Transsexual?

Feel like a man in a woman's body or a woman in a man's body? Identify with the opposite sex? Is there a third or fourth gender?

The definition of a transgender person includes the following: One who identifies with a gender other than the biological gender into which they were born. The definition can include persons who deviate in one way or another from their cultural gender roles, and many subcategories.

A transsexual may be generally defined as: A person with a psychological urge to belong to the opposite sex that may be carried to the point of undergoing surgery to modify the sex organs to mimic the opposite sex. A transsexual seems to be defined more by an inner urge to carry on a change outwardly, and wants to live as the opposite sex.

Note these definitions are in flux. The very fact that they are so fluid and involved tells us something. There are so many concepts of gender identity, blending of genders (third and fourth genders), and sexual orientation expressed in these general categories, that it would take an in-depth and professional study to understand all the positions held by the interested communities.

Some have said that a transgender or transsexual person suffers from gender identity disorder. Others may say that is perfectly natural for who they are. That is how they were born. Natural "fallen-ness" and God's design are two different things. I do not doubt anyone's deepest longings or feelings, but the Word of God deals with, among other things: (1) conduct, (2) the change of the sin nature, (3) transformation of the inner person—heart, mind, will, desires, and emotions through Christ, (4) embracing creative design, and (5) God's purpose and identity for our lives in the image of Christ.

There are a variety of theories on the source of gender identity disorder. One is that there is hormonal cause that hinders or alters gender development of the baby in the womb. Emotional influences before birth or certainly in early childhood development may be causes. But that does not alter God's ultimate purpose, truth, and design. It does not alter what the Lord can do by His grace and power, or what such persons should refrain from doing by His grace and power. I am going to review this subject from a scriptural perspective.

There was a man in the Bible who was born blind. When Jesus's disciples asked whose fault it was, Jesus said it wasn't anyone's fault. Jesus then proceeded to anoint the man's eyes with clay made out of His spit and dirt. Jesus made this profound statement in John 9:5: "As long as I am in the world, I am the light of the world." The message: As long as Jesus was around, He was going to bring light, order, healing, and truth. Light does not hide itself. He is the Light of the World. The man washed his eyes and came back seeing (John 9:7).

I think we need to realize in this story that while Jesus obviously did not condemn the man for being blind, Jesus didn't congratulate him either or pretend that there wasn't a problem. This would be a mixed message for all ages. The message would be that God isn't in the healing business; or that God isn't in any business at all; or He should stay out of our business; or that we should celebrate lack, sickness, and blindness, and be blind to the fact that it is a minus instead of a plus. Everything is God's business, from creation to redemption to judgment, from heaven to hell. He is the great Lover, Lord, Life, and Law of the universe. Yet, He will not force Himself into our lives—the man still had to accept the healing here and take steps to receive it. What a great blessing if we only receive from Him, whatever our brokenness.

The Father's heart grieves when His creation is bruised, wounded, confused, or less than the wholeness intended, whether eyes, ears, infirmity, or desire to be another gender. It wasn't the blind man's fault here, but it wasn't the Creator's intent or design either. Our emotional disposition is shaped by many factors, but we are all born sinners, we are all born morally ill. King David wrote, "Behold, I was brought forth in iniquity, and in sin my mother conceived me" (Ps. 51:5, NKJV). It is God's desire to bring all persons back to the wholeness and holiness He intended.

Also, going back to the man born blind, in order to be made whole, he had to believe Jesus for his sight and take the steps of obedience to be healed. The man born blind had never seen light. In a way, he didn't know what was missing, but he trusted in the Master to give "sight" to his life on this issue. Assume a transgender/transsexual doesn't know what he or she is missing in the wholeness of their gender, or fiercely insists that he or she feels more like the other gender; that person still must trust in God's Word and provision. This is a disaster and a tragedy of epic proportions. Gender "disidentification" is a broken condition. Somewhere along the line we all have to believe that God has a better and final plan.

Jesus was roundly criticized by the religious leaders for this healing, and He told them that they were blind, because they said that they could see. They refused to acknowledge their spiritual blindness, and therefore they stayed in darkness. But the man born blind was able to see (spiritually and naturally) because he received that healing by faith from Jesus.

Jesus is the missing part of our life in every area, and He gives hope, heals, and defines the path of obedience and restoration. No person can change himself or herself, but the Holy Spirit changes lives.

Jesus said He had come as the Light of the World. It was His divine desire that we should see Him and our true condition, so that we could be changed as He, the Creator, directs by His will and our choice.

Let's extend this concept to the creative order in as described in the Word of God. The Bible says male and female created He them. Mark 10:6 says, "But from the beginning of the creation God made them male and female." This is God's creation and order. He created male and female, and He made no mistakes, and He blessed male and female. If a person was born with a male body, that was God's plan. If a person was born with a female body, that was God's plan. "Male and female created He them" is an important phrase in the scripture, because the male was the man and the female was the woman at creation. It wasn't "male and female created He him (Adam)," or a blended notion of gender or cross-gender concept.

God's creative intent is expressed in Psalm 139:13–16 (NLT):

> You made all the delicate, inner parts of my body, and knit me together in my mother's womb. Thank you for making me so wonderfully complex! Your workmanship is marvelous—and how well I know it. You watched me as I was being formed in utter seclusion, as I was woven together in the dark of the womb. You saw me before I was born. Every day of my life was recorded in your book. Every moment was laid out before a single day had passed.

The King James Version writes verse 16 like this:

> Thine eyes did see my substance, yet being unperfect; and in thy book all my members were written, which

in continuance were fashioned, when as yet there was
none of them.

The Scriptures state that the Lord knew every part of you as you were being formed. Notice verse 13 says "of my body," not "emotions or desires." You were no surprise to God as your body parts were formed in "utter seclusion." The Psalm says that in "His book"—God's record of your life—all "my members were written." Therefore, every member of your body was recorded by God in advance. God's creative plan was made in advance. To add or subtract from the body in order to change gender alters what was in the heart and mind of God—actually written in a book—for each person from creation. To disregard what God has created also is in contrast to creative order. (Not talking about "intersex" persons here where a gender determination must be made.)

Isaiah 44:24 (THE MESSAGE) says, "God, your Redeemer, who shaped your life in your mother's womb, says: 'I am God. I made all that is. With no help from you I spread out the skies and laid out the earth.'" God made you. He formed us in the womb. We are creation. He is Creator. He is God.

The Lord told the prophet Jeremiah, "I knew you before I formed you in your mother's womb. Before you were born I set you apart and appointed you as my spokesman to the world" (Jer. 1:5, NLT).

God had a plan for Jeremiah before his body was even created in his mother's womb, and this is true for all of us.

Your true identity and destiny were established by God before you ever entered this planet. That doesn't mean these cannot be aborted or distorted, but it is not God's will.

What if Jeremiah had said, "I feel like a female in a male's body"? His destiny was set before he even had body parts, just as in every life, to align with the will of God and the Word of God by the power of God.

It is the nature of fallen man to resist what God has created.

> Destruction is certain for those who argue with their Creator. Does a clay pot ever argue with its maker? Does the clay dispute with the one who shapes it, saying, "Stop, you are doing it wrong!" Does the pot exclaim, "How clumsy can you be!" How terrible it would be if a newborn baby said to its father and mother, "Why was I born? Why did you make me this way?"
>
> —Isaiah 45:9–10, nlt

Our fallen and broken state brings dissatisfaction. There is emptiness. The human race is always looking for a change or "fix" that will bring a solution to torment, sadness, emptiness, and craving. This search may not be a conscious one at all times, but it is compelling.

However, in the end, that change we all need is the love of God and the transforming power of the Holy Spirit, not self-inflicted injury by a sex change. The Bible tells a story in Mark chapter 5 of a man of Gadara. He was demonized, and spent his entire time crying, living in the tombs, and cutting himself with stones. Yes, there were spirits that drove him to mutilate himself. He exhibited patterns of self-hatred, isolation from the community, depression, self-destruction, and sorrow. Therefore, might not some similar spirits be operating with those who want to change their original gender? However, the demonized man put himself under the Lordship of Jesus Christ and his life was transformed. At the end of the story he is clothed and in his right mind. While the man wanted to follow Jesus in His travels, in verse 19 (nlt), Jesus said, "No, go home to your friends, and tell them what wonderful things the Lord has done for you and how merciful he has been." The Lord does do wonderful things and He is merciful.

The "transsexual" or "transgender," like all persons on this planet, needs to be "transformed" by the creative and redeeming power of God, not the surgeon's knife, or other outward appearance.

God wants us born again from within, not rearranged from without. Being "born again" means that your spirit is born again from above that it may partake of the divine nature and do the will of God in the body you were given. Scripture tells us that we will receive resurrection bodies. How does this work with the transsexual? I believe the person is going to be in the form in which he or she was originally designed. A believer is not coming back as a female if born male. Of course we need to remember the conditions of Scripture for resurrection in bodily form.

The Lord tells us that the outer man is perishing day by day. This is not the most important part of our identity anyway; it the house we live in. We are spirit beings, with a soul, who live in a body.

> Therefore we do not lose heart. Even though our outward man is perishing, yet the inward man is being renewed day by day.
>
> —2 Corinthians 4:16, nkjv

A person can rearrange all the pieces of his or her life with gender reassignment surgery, implants, hormones, and so forth, but that does not change the inner person who is in need of a Savior, who needs to be born again and renewed to grow in the image of Jesus Christ. The outer part, our physical tent, is to conform to God's plan of holiness. God is a holy God, and says, "Be ye holy, for I am holy" (Lev. 20:7).

The Cross does not exist to affirm the desires of the fallen nature or the flesh. The Father wants all of us to grow into the image of His Son, and honor Him as Lord. When our spirit and soul are under the Lordship of Jesus Christ, by choice we will yield our members as instruments of righteousness. (See Romans 6.) Yes, the Lord cares about our needs and desires—He provides for us, and has determined a sexual and gender order according to His Word.

"But I feel like a woman," or "I feel like a man," or both. It seems that there is a woman in this man's body, or a man in this woman's body, or a greater identification with the opposite gender. If those cravings are not God's will, where would that powerful desire come from? Here are some answers from the spiritual side:

There are perverse spirits that pass through generations, such as female or male demonic entities, that want to "express" themselves in a body. These are impersonating spirits that want to "act out" their own identities. They have no body in which to dwell, so they are seeking a human in which to live out their desires.

There may be occult practices in the family line, and a male or female demonic "god" or "goddess" is passed through the generations to even a little child, who feels like a member of the opposite sex (or both sexes). There may be practices in pagan religions that encourage crossing to another gender or gender blurring behavior.

Spirits can also cause individuals to hate who they are. "Self-hatred" interacts with "rebellion" and "rejection," "insecurity," and "inferiority" to distort and pervert true identity.

Emotionally, self-hatred can accumulate in a child's heart when parents do not love, nurture, strengthen, and help children to grow in the way that the Lord intends.

There are traumas, even small ones, and perceptions and judgments of a child that can cause an individual to flee from his or her gender in pain and fear. All the reasons why people think they are born a certain way are in operation here.

Perhaps we can add to that possible sexual abuse, absent parents, parents that reject their child's gender or add to confusion, lack of bonding, and environmental encouragement. This level of self-rejection and self-hatred is deep and intense. It takes the power of the blood of Jesus and the Holy Spirit to bring freedom through deliverance, prayer, and counseling.

What of the possible physical causes? God still has a design and plan for such persons. The Lord is still the Healer. Go back to the man born blind.

One big word on self-hatred, self-rejection, and shame: Man's original sin was to seek an identity apart from God. When he did that, Adam and Eve realized they were naked and were ashamed. So shame was the first result of sin. Lifestyles apart from God's intended order and creation, as He shows us in His Word, will always result in shame on the inside, no matter how much societal acceptance or legal validation is given. There is an innate sense of shame when a person does not fulfill who they are, and this is for all people. Only God has the roadmap. A life with a true foundation is based on the Word of God and obedience. A life with a false foundation is based on the sin nature and eventually produces sorrow and death. The Bible promises us a true life rooted and grounded in love (Eph. 3:17), and producing love, joy, peace, longsuffering, gentleness, goodness, faith, meekness, temperance: against such there is no law (Gal. 5:22–23).

The transgender/transsexual has internally, perhaps without great awareness or intentional rebellion, rejected a God-given identity. As a result, there is a "double whammy" of shame: Shame that their true identity is a failure, faulty, not workable, not "good enough" as a male or female. Additionally there is shame in the acting out this brokenness—ashamed of their true identities and ashamed of their false ones. Only the devil could put a person in such bondage, for he is the father of lies.

When Paul the Apostle found himself in a situation where he could not be free, he cried out: "O wretched man that I am! who shall deliver me from the body of this death?" (Rom. 7:24). But God has an answer in the next chapter: "There is therefore now no condemnation to them which are in Christ Jesus, who walk not after the flesh, but after the Spirit. For the law of the Spirit of life in Christ Jesus hath made me free from the law of sin and death" (Rom. 8:1–2).

Please know that *no one* can live according to the Word of God and God's intended design and purpose without the new birth, the power of the Holy Spirit, and understanding the Word of God deep in our hearts—truth in the inward parts.

Part IV
OTHER CONDUCT

PORNOGRAPHY

INTERNET PORN, HARD core and soft core pornographic movies, virtual online sexual relations, strip clubs, and so forth are common entertainment and experiences in our culture. Fantasy sex introduces perverse and unclean spirits that are operating in that movie, activity, or other media. Lust does not bring love. Lust is never satisfied anyway. Love grows through sacrifice, commitment, communication, intimacy, sharing, forgiveness—real things like that.

With regard to the married person, getting to know your spouse and communicating in a mature way (maybe even get help, healing, counsel, and deliverance), is harder to do than watch some porn or go to a club, but the results of this process are eternal, and you will have a solid relationship rather than lustful experience fueled by fantasy. You may not even get that!

For the unmarried, there are the same considerations. In addition to the sinful component of these practices, porn and other sexual encounters or experiences out of the will of God, whether real or virtual, are not the road to maturity; they do not aid in learning to communicate or deal with the harder issues of life. Porn and other such sexual encounters or experiences do not prepare young men or women for marriage, it just ruins them. Unfortunately, children and young people are massively exposed to porn. Such experiences become addictive. Sexual fantasy, vicarious gratification, non-committed sexual experiences, and the like take a person further and further away from true life, from themselves, God's promises and destiny—and, as a bonus, transfer demonic spirits.

But for those who need Scripture on this one, this comes straight from *Jesus Himself*:

> But I say unto you, That whosoever looketh on a woman to lust after her hath committed adultery with her already in his heart. And if thy right eye offend thee, pluck it out, and cast it from thee; for it is profitable for thee that one of thy members should perish, and not that thy whole body should be cast into hell.
>
> —MATTHEW 5:28–29

Before there was a name for it, Jesus was talking here about the sin of fantasy sex, looking at a woman or man with lust, long before Internet porn, as one example, came along. And His solution was extreme.

What is God's solution? As in all sin, repentance and asking the Lord for forgiveness is a start. There may also be a process of healing, deliverance, and restoration that is necessary. Jesus said that a person's eternity is worth more than human vision. Pornographic and sexual images do not depart quickly—there are spirits operating with and attached to these images— that is why they stick and have such power. If you have been exposed to porn and sexual images you may need to be delivered (from demonic oppression) and healed.

God's intent is that we look at people with the eyes of Jesus, to love them, serve them, and lead them closer to the Lord, not use them for self-gratification.

There was a king named David. One day he was taking a stroll on the rooftop of his palace and he saw a woman named Bathsheba taking a bath. She was very beautiful—he obviously lusted after her body. He had her brought over to his house and had sex with her. She got pregnant. However, there was a hitch—Bathsheba was married to another man,

Uriah. Because of David's sin and Bathsheba's pregnancy, he arranged for Uriah to be killed in battle. Not very noble for a king, especially one that seemed so close to God. However, lust is powerful, and lust is ignited by what we see. When lust is combined with what we do, sin is born, and the end of that sin is death.

James 1:13–15 (NKJV) says:

> Let no one say when he is tempted, "I am tempted by God"; for God cannot be tempted by evil, nor does He Himself tempt anyone. But each one is tempted when he is drawn away by his own desires and enticed. Then, when desire has conceived, it gives birth to sin; and sin, when it is full-grown, brings forth death.

What happened in this story, which was a lust story, as opposed to a love story? David suffered severe consequences in his own family because of that sin. He lost the infant son born of Bathsheba who was conceived through the adultery. Another son of his raped one of his daughters (from another wife), and an internal war was started in the family, brother against brother, that lasted a very long time, ending in the death of two sons. God worked His redemption out in the situation, but it was a brutal, hard time for David. There was civil war, and he almost lost his kingdom. It caused him and others a lot of grief. Many people died because of David's sin; he wasn't the only person who reaped the consequences of a little sexual fantasy acted out. Especially if you are the head of a family, a little sin will not just cost you, but your wife, children, and perhaps grandchildren will feel its effects. It may even cost you your home, marriage, finances, health, or life. Is it worth it?

> Don't be misled. Remember that you can't ignore God and get away with it. You will always reap what you sow! Those who live only to satisfy their own sinful desires will harvest the consequences of decay

and death. But those who live to please the Spirit will harvest everlasting life from the Spirit. So don't get tired of doing what is good. Don't get discouraged and give up, for we will reap a harvest of blessing at the appropriate time.

—Galatians 6:7–9, nlt

Job said, "I made a covenant with mine eyes; why then should I think upon a maid?" (Job 31:1). Job determined that his eyes would not be used for purposes of lust.

An antidote to lust—purity of heart. Pleasing God by purity of heart, a higher goal, will take you over lust. Fix your eyes on the prize.

MASTURBATION

There is nothing in the Bible that covers masturbation, but by nature it involves sexual fantasy and it isolates individuals, as opposed to joining them—which is God's design and intent for sexuality. For that reason, in principle, it does not reflect God's ways or God's purpose for sexuality. Masturbation is also highly addictive—the inevitable outcome for people who watch porn and get aroused and/or relieve themselves on their own for whatever reasons, whenever they want. What are the boundaries here? Having a hard day? Bored? Wound up? Need comfort and pleasure? First Timothy 3 talks about people who are "lovers of themselves." An excellent book dealing with such issues is *The Anatomy of Seduction* by Jack W. Hayford, pastoral leader and author.

ORAL/ANAL SEX

First remember that God's plan for sexual expression is in marriage—whatever the practice may be. Both mentioned above are sexual activities. (There is no waiver to the effect that oral sex is "not sex"—note to the unmarried.) But even in marriage, there are some things to consider: The fact that some sexual activities are damaging to the body and in contrast to the design of the body; the question of whether the practice supports the emotional intimacy, mutual passion, and the oneness God intends in sexual intercourse; and finally, whether both parties genuinely want to perform these activities. Even with the liberty of the sexual relationship in marriage, the marriage bed is not to be defiling. (Heb. 13:4). Some questions to ask: Does each party want to do this, feel comfortable with such practices, and does the Holy Spirit in each spouse bear witness to this?

To quote Jack W. Hayford from his book, *Sex and the Single Soul*, "I have never been in a counseling situation in which I've found that either of these practices contributed to the fulfillment of the marriage. Instead, I have dealt with many, many cases in which they have distracted from the highest satisfaction of the husband and wife's union"[1]. He also discusses the invasion of the "world-spirit" into our intimate lives.[2]

> What? know ye not that your body is the temple of the Holy Ghost which is in you, which ye have of God, and ye are not your own? For ye are bought with a price: therefore glorify God in your body, and in your spirit, which are God's.
>
> —1 CORINTHIANS 6:19–20

INCEST

What about having sexual relations with a family member or marrying a close family member? It seems that even from the Bible, Cain must have married his sister, and Abraham married Sarah, his half sister.

Let's take this one step at a time:

1. All sexual relations outside of marriage are sinful—between anyone; brother, sister, friends, with strangers, with prostitutes, and so forth.

2. If sexual relations are forbidden, what about marriage to close relatives? To answer this we

look to the law of the land, and Scripture. The law of the land and the law of God have placed boundaries on sexual relations.

3. *Webster's Dictionary* defines incest as "sexual intercourse between persons so closely related that they are forbidden by law to marry." It is the law of the land that close relations not marry or have sexual relations. This would clearly be brother and sister, father, daughter, mother, son; even close cousins, aunts, nephews, uncles, and nieces.

4. Under the law of most states marrying close relatives is unlawful.

5. Even though early in Bible history there appears to be no prohibition with brothers and sisters marrying, at some point in time, God put a stop to this, and His will is seen in the law of Moses. (It is also likely, by further conjecture, that the human race genetically became more and more weakened in sickness and sin; therefore, incest would have detrimental effects on children as time passed.)

With regard to incest the list is long here:

You must never have sexual intercourse with a close relative, for I am the Lord.

Do not violate your father by having sexual intercourse with your mother. She is your mother; you must never have intercourse with her.

Do not have sexual intercourse with any of your father's wives, for this would violate your father.

Do not have sexual intercourse with your sister or half sister, whether she is your father's daughter or

your mother's daughter, whether she was brought up
in the same family or somewhere else.

Do not have sexual intercourse with your
granddaughter, whether your son's daughter or your
daughter's daughter; that would violate you.

Do not have sexual intercourse with the daughter
of any of your father's wives; she is your half sister.

Do not have intercourse with your aunt, your
father's sister, because she is your father's close
relative.

Do not have sexual intercourse with your aunt,
your mother's sister, because she is your mother's
close relative.

And do not violate your uncle, your father's brother,
by having sexual intercourse with his wife; she also is
your aunt.

Do not have sexual intercourse with your daughter-
in-law; she is your son's wife.

Do not have intercourse with your brother's wife;
this would violate your brother.

Do not have sexual intercourse with both a woman
and her daughter or marry both a woman and her
granddaughter, whether her son's daughter or her
daughter's daughter. They are close relatives, and to
do this would be a horrible wickedness.

Do not marry a woman and her sister because they
will be rivals. But if your wife dies, then it is all right
to marry her sister.

—Leviticus 18:6–18, nlt

The operative phrase is "do not."
Deuteronomy 27:20–23 (nlt) also says:

Cursed is anyone who has sexual intercourse with
his father's wife, for he has violated his father. And
all the people will reply, "Amen." Cursed is anyone
who has sexual intercourse with an animal. And all

the people will reply, "Amen." Cursed is anyone who has sexual intercourse with his sister, whether she is the daughter of his father or his mother. And all the people will reply, "Amen." Cursed is anyone who has sexual intercourse with his mother-in-law. And all the people will reply, "Amen."

The operative result is "cursed."

Let us also consider the trauma of an older family member having sexual relations with a younger or another family member, the type of control that occurs in such situations, and the helplessness of the child or younger member. This causes all kinds of "curses" in the families that continues for generations. This is how lives are ruined.

Which takes us into the next topic—Is it acceptable to have sexual relations with a child? Why not, if they are consenting?

Sexual Relations with a Child

First of all, sexual relations with a child are highly damaging to the emotional life of the child—my view, after praying for a lot of people who are now adults. This is the beginning of a lifetime disaster. It is not ever, and never will be, acceptable to have adult/child sexual relations, no matter what arguments are given concerning the child's consent, or even that the child seemed to want the sexual encounter (such as, the child seduced the older participant—I have heard this). Children cannot give informed consent; children are de facto at the mercy of an adult. The adult has the responsibility to abide by godly and healthy boundaries. The encounter will inevitably cause guilt and shame to the child.

Second, just in an automatic generic sense using the original pattern, all sexual relations outside of marriage are sinful whether with children, infants, adults, or young teenagers. It is clear that five, eight, ten-year-old children do not marry (at least not in Western cultures), and it is usually not the intent of an older person to "marry" a five or eight or ten-year-old person when they initiate sexual contact. I know this sounds preposterous, but just want to clarify the pattern.

People who want to have sexual relations with children are usually emotionally damaged themselves, and certainly are not fulfilling the commands of God's love. Perverse spirits are in operation as well as the imprinted sinful patterns of their own damage.

Jesus summed it up when He said in Matthew 18:6: "But whoso shall offend one of these little ones which believe in me, it were better for him that a millstone were hanged about his neck, and that he were drowned in the depth of the sea."

Why, because the offense to a little one damages his or her life forever. The emotional trauma is great and stops healthy growth and a child's trust of others and God. This will be an "offense" to a child that could change a child's destiny for eternity, perhaps an eternity in hell instead of heaven.

Under the law of all states, an older person who has intercourse with a child or an underage person will be considered committing "statutory rape." In other words, even if there is consent, it is against the law; by statute it is wrong.

Also, under the law of various states, individuals must be a certain age to marry unless parental consent is given

CROSS-DRESSING

The woman shall not wear that which pertains unto a man, neither shall a man put on a woman's garment: for all that do so are abomination unto the LORD thy God.

—DEUTERONOMY 22:5

A woman must not wear men's clothing, and a man must not wear women's clothing. The LORD your God detests people who do this.

—DEUTERONOMY 22:5, NLT

I am going to interpret that as wearing clothes specifically designed for the opposite sex—such as brassieres and panty hose, and/or deliberately dressing to look like the opposite sex. For example, women and girls in Western society wear pants. That doesn't mean that they are cross-dressers. A cross-dresser intentionally wants to look like the opposite sex, and may also change their appearance with makeup, hairstyle, and other effects. A person can have a desire to be a cross-dresser from an early age. Many people have desire in this area, and such a desire does not originate with God, because it is not confirmed by the Word of God. There are deep psychological reasons for cross-dressing that need to be uncovered and released to God in repentance, forgiveness, and deliverance.

ADULTERY

This is very clear in scriptures: "Thou shalt not commit adultery" (Exod. 20:14). As stated in the beginning of this book, exclusivity in the marriage relationship is ordained of God—two people bonded together as one person in the covenant of marriage with sexual exclusivity.

INORDINATE AFFECTION

The Bible also describes "inordinate affection"—this can occur between any combination of people with or without consent of all persons. It is affection that is excessive, out of boundaries, ill-regulated, not set in order. The King James Version of the Bible says this in Colossians 3:5–7:

> Mortify therefore your members which are upon the earth; fornication, uncleanness, inordinate affection, evil concupiscence, and covetousness, which is idolatry: For which things' sake the wrath of God cometh on the children of disobedience: In the which ye also walked some time, when ye lived in them.

Colossians 3:3–7 in the Message Bible gives another perspective as well:

> Your old life is dead. Your new life, which is your real life—even though invisible to spectators—is with Christ in God. He is your life. When Christ (your real life, remember) shows up again on this earth, you'll show up, too—the real you, the glorious you. Meanwhile, be content with obscurity, like Christ. And that means killing off everything connected with that way of death: sexual promiscuity, impurity, lust, doing whatever you feel like whenever you feel like it, and grabbing whatever attracts your fancy. That's a life shaped by things and feelings instead of by God. It's because of this kind of thing that God is about to explode in anger. It wasn't long ago that you were doing all that stuff and not knowing any better.

OTHERS

There are many practices in the world originating from the human imagination. Let's just remember this: We are not objects nor are we to treat others as objects, but we are children of God. God set a simple and holy pattern between man and woman in marriage. The more complicated it gets, the further it departs from God's pattern, blessing, and reality.

Part V

ABORTION—A TRAGEDY FOR ALL

A RE THERE UNWANTED children? Not with God. Jesus said, "Suffer the little children, and forbid them not, to come unto me: for of such is the kingdom of heaven" (Matt. 19:14).

Exodus 20:13: "Thou shall not kill." Many times the Word of God says that Lord knew a child from his mother's womb. What if that child had been aborted? What would happen to all the divine potential? John the Baptist, in the womb of his mother, Elizabeth, leaped with joy when Mary, pregnant with Jesus, came to visit Elizabeth: Two fetuses communicating by the Spirit. There is another realm greater than our flesh or soul realm—the spirit realm—which is at operation in our lives even before we are born. (Refer to Mother Theresa's message on abortion at the 1994 National Prayer Breakfast, where she discusses this divine meeting.[1] It is very profound reading.)

We are made in the image of God, and that is why Satan loves abortion. It is an opportunity to stop the divine possibilities of the only creature made in the image of the Creator, and the only creature that will bring his ultimate downfall. We see in scripture the plans of Pharaoh and Herod to destroy the male babies—why, to cut off godly seed that could restore a nation or save a world. Where does human life start? That is the question. For many of us, we confirm and believe it starts at conception, and that the child has the right to its own life upon conception. If it wasn't life, why would it continue to grow?

Mother Teresa called it a "war against the child."[2] I recommend that the readers of this book read what she has to say. One of the main reasons for abortion is simply unwanted pregnancy (no issue with life or health of mother, defects in child, rape, or incest, or an elective abortion). Women may abort their babies because at the time, having a baby would cause shame or inconvenience. Some people want to cover their sin or mistake. Some want to get out of a mess at the time. Or they don't want to face the time or expense of raising a child at the time. Perhaps they don't want to be linked with that sexual partner for the next several years. Perhaps they are exhausted from other children at the time. At the time they may be incapable of raising a child—immaturity, economic conditions, and the like. Now there is even selective abortion, when one of perhaps three embryos in the womb can be aborted. There is abortion for sex selection in some countries. The reasons for the "choice" of aborting the baby are many. But what choice does the baby have (a separate human being, with a different set of DNA than the mother)? And what about the pain that the fetus experiences, who may be sucked out of the uterus, chopped up, or have its skull crushed, among other things.

The reasons for abortion due to an unwanted pregnancy can be very strong and compelling at the time. I don't want to minimize the trauma, fear, shock, shame, or dread a woman may experience in this life-altering situation. However, although the pregnancy may be unwanted and traumatic, like a lot of other things in life, the solution is not to kill another human being, an innocent human being. In fact, later on in life that woman may wish with all her heart she had not ended the life of her child. The abortion is traumatic for the child. Unfortunately, abortion is simply a form of birth control in the United States. Let's face it, more than 50 million dead babies in America is not just about the life and health of the mother, defects in the child, rape, or incest, but one of the disastrous end results of the sexual revolution. As Mother Teresa said: "Any country that accepts abortion is not teaching the people to love, but to use any violence to get what they want."[3] As difficult as it is, believers are called to self-control and responsibility. This is revival ground. Changed hearts and changed lives means changed behavior in accordance with the Word of God. In point of fact, we don't control birth; another life has been created. Abortion is not going to stop because of any of the arguments against it. It is going to stop when lives are transformed by God.

Results of Abortion

An abortion increases the chances of sterility. Abortion has been linked to breast cancer, according to some studies, and can surely cause mental and emotional distress for the mother, not to mention the taking of an innocent life.[4] There are always consequences to abortion. The guilt, shame, hurt, and pain of abortion can last in a lifetime unless and until the process of repentance, forgiveness, and inner healing occurs. And even if there is emotional distance from this event, does anyone ever forget it? Abortion is performed and undertaken very casually in the United States, and I believe that has brought judgment on this land.

Redemption

For those of you who have had an abortion, or your wife or girlfriend has aborted your child at your request or by your influence, or you have facilitated an abortion in some way; God has not turned His back on you. That is why Jesus went to the Cross.

Solution

First, repent. Ask forgiveness from the Lord and others. Break the curse of abortion and death and the trauma of abortion over your life. Release the child to God. Ask the Lord to heal your heart. Many people have written books to minister to those who have been impacted by abortion. There are whole ministries dedicated to this area. Seek these out. Others have been through this. Remember God is merciful and forgiving, He is the Healer and Deliverer. There is nothing that a person has done that cannot be forgiven. He restores our souls and lives.

Birth Defects, Rape, and Incest

If we are of the opinion that life starts at conception, it would be no more valid to kill a child who is the product of rape or incest or will possibly have birth defects, before birth, than it would be after birth. The basic issue is the right to life. If that is settled, then it is settled for all, and all parties, mother and child, are to be treated with compassion and given equal rights.

Life or Health of Mother

With regard to the life of the mother it is going to be an issue of conscience, and weighing the alternatives, as to whose life is to prevail. I think it is clear that if there is truly an issue of life, then the life of the mother can prevail in good conscience. But when we consider the "health" of the mother, what kind of health is being considered? Emotional health, distress, or what? Further, there are situations when an abortion is recommended by a doctor because medicine the mother is required to take may harm the baby, or the mother's physical condition can cause harm to the baby. I think we must differentiate between the baby dying as caused by the condition or medicine, as opposed to preemptively aborting the baby.

YOU ASK, WHAT about my sexual needs? Turn your needs over to God. Be filled with His life. Do His will no matter what the personal cost. Take up your cross daily and follow Him by obeying Him and pleasing Him for eternal purposes. This does not make you asexual (without sexual feeling) or non-sexual, it just makes you celibate, or abstaining from sex. You are not dropping out, giving up, or succumbing to passivity. You are obeying the Lord—as in *any* other area of life.

When we are filled with God, we can transition from a self-centered life to a God-centered life, which is what the Lord wants for everyone, unmarried or married, anyway. We become filled with the joy and the presence of God. God knows our needs and is interested in sending a person to fulfill them; but to be honest, His eternal purposes and our walk of holiness are ultimately bigger than momentary needs. His timing is going to rule. Our lives are bigger than our lives. I believe that walking with the Lord in this area takes great faith in the Word of God, and great strength by the power of the Holy Spirit. However, it is worth it. Blessed are the pure in heart, for they shall see God (Matt. 5:8).

God knows *how* and *when* to answer prayers. Make yourself ready for marriage, if this is what you desire. But even if that isn't your desire, or you cannot comprehend it as your desire, Jesus calls us to follow Him, be holy, humble, submitted, broken, and open. Allow the Spirit of God to rule and direct every area of your life, including your sexuality.

God created you, loves you, and knows what is best for you.

That is why He is God. Every cell in our bodies, every piece of matter, originates with Him. He has the pattern for living. It all fits together when we trust Him for what is best in our lives.

> Those who are wise will shine as bright as the sky, and those who turn many to righteousness will shine like stars forever.
>
> —Daniel 12:3, NLT

BEFORE WE GET started on these, I want to offer the ultimate invitation that God, the Father, Son, and Holy Spirit has offered to us, from the foundation of the world, the opportunity of salvation and an eternal relationship with God through the sacrifice of His Son, Jesus Christ on the cross, where He took our sins. Perhaps you have never said this prayer or you have said something like it before, but want to rededicate your life. Here is God's opportunity for you:

Dear Heavenly Father, I ask Jesus Christ into my heart to be my Lord and Savior. I know I am a sinner, but I believe the blood of Jesus cleanses me from all sin. I repent of my sins. Come into my heart, Lord Jesus, and make me a new creation. I give You all of my life, and ask for all of Yours. Fill me, O Lord, with Your Spirit, and absorb my life into Yours, that I may glorify You. In Jesus's name, amen.

REPENTANCE/RENOUNCING/BREAKING CURSES/SOUL TIES AND COVENANTS

Dear Heavenly Father, I repent on behalf of myself and the generations before me, on my mother's side of the family, and on my father's side of the family. I repent for all sexual sin, including fornication, adultery, pornography, homosexuality, and lesbianism [add others as necessary, such as rape, incest, prostitution, ritual sex, cross-dressing], and for all patterns of sexual sin, multiple marriages and generations of fornication.

I renounce all such sin, and repent of such sin in my own life, and I break all generational curses in the area of fornication, adultery, pornography, homosexuality, lesbianism, rape, incest, prostitution, cross-dressing, transgendered and transsexual lifestyles [name others] in my life.

I command all spirits of fornication, uncleanness, homosexuality, pornography, adultery, impersonating spirits [add others; possibly false identity] to leave me. I give You this false identity and ask for my true identity. I acknowledge that I am [male or female].

I break all ungodly soul ties and ungodly covenants with those whom I have had sexual relations or experiences with, outside of marriage. [You can name these people, and explicitly break ties with them. This might also include ties to strip clubs (places), objects/toys—whatever they may be, pornographic or erotic images or virtual sex—anything else the Holy Spirit quickens, whether real people are involved or not. You can do this in other areas of life too.]

Lord, I ask You to return to me all fragments of my soul that have been torn away by ungodly soul ties in sexual relationships and experiences outside of marriage.

I repent of and renounce ungodly forms of sex [list what is in your heart]. I break ties with these practices, and renounce them.

Forgive [me and/or the generations before me] for having children outside of marriage. Lord, I break generational patterns and curses of illegitimacy, and I consecrate my children to You. I break patterns of divorce in the family line as well.

Release me and cleanse me from the shame that pulls down my life and heart. I know You love me and I receive Your love for me.

FORGIVENESS AND BREAKING OF SOUL TIES—MOLESTATION, RAPE, ABUSE

I forgive those [name these people] who have sexually used me and molested me, raped, and abused me. I break all ungodly soul ties with those who have used me, molested me, raped or abused me.

Dear Lord, cleanse me from fear, grief, heartache, self-hatred, hatred, anger, rage, hatred of [men/ women]. I forgive myself for being used, and I forgive my [mother/father] for not protecting me.

I break in the name of Jesus all evil power, possession, and control of [name person] over me, and every ungodly soul tie between me and [name person] in the area of [abuse, etc.]. Dear Lord, restore my soul and return to me all of my soul tied to that person in an ungodly way.

I repent for all sins in the family line, on my mother's side of the family, and my father's side of the family, of rape, incest, sexual abuse [name whatever], and I ask You, Lord, to break these curses in my family line.

I command unclean spirits of molestation, rape, abuse, grief, rejection, incest, abandonment, heartache, death, and perversion to leave me. I command every spirit of trauma and fear to leave me.

Release me and cleanse me from the shame that pulls down my life and heart.

ESPECIALLY FOR AFRICAN AMERICANS

I forgive those who separated and destroyed black families as a result of slavery and other societal and government interference. I forgive and release them, and I break the curse of separation, divorce, and detachment over my family. I forgive those who used and abused my slave ancestors sexually, and I break the curses of such captivity and oppression. I know You love me and I receive Your love for me. I command every spirit of trauma to leave me.

For Homosexuality/Lesbianism

Dear Heavenly Father, I repent of [homosexuality/ lesbianism]. I know it is a sin. I renounce these practices, and I ask You, Lord, to remake my life in the image of Your Son. Give me an identity in You. I forgive those who introduced me to homosexual practices, or molested me. I forgive myself.

I break generational curses of homosexuality and lesbianism in my life, and I repent on behalf of my family, on my mother's side of the family, and my father's side of the family, for such sins.

I command all homosexual spirits, spirits of rejection, rebellion, trauma and fear, to leave me and other unclean spirits [name them as the Holy Spirit reveals].

I break every ungodly soul tie and covenant with those [men or women] with whom I have had a homosexual/lesbian relationship. I break false covenants and commitments. I renounce any false marriage or partnership.

I ask You, Lord, to rise up in me and give me strength to walk as Your Son walked. Release me and cleanse me from the shame and pain that pulls down my life and heart. Fill in the gaps in my emotional life, or the gaps in my gender identity, by Your creative Holy Spirit. I ask forgiveness for rejecting myself and how You have designed me.

*Work in my life that I may reclaim my true iden-
tity, break down the barriers I have had in my heart
to my [father or mother]. I forgive my same sex
parent for abandoning, neglecting, or abusing me,
and not releasing to me my true identity. Take away
those defenses that I have used to protect and control
my life and emotions. Set me free. I know You love
me and I receive Your love for me.*

[For those who have engaged in homosexuality or lesbianism, it is valuable to receive deliverance, mind renewal,
counseling, and prayers for inner healing.]

SEE ALSO ABOVE: TRANSSEXUALS/ TRANSGENDERED

[For those who are have changed their bodily identity, have
become transsexuals, or want to change gender or believe they
are another gender, it is valuable to repent of self-hatred, muti-
lation, deception, and pretending to be someone else. Also,
cast out and break agreement with any impersonating male or
female spirit. Ask the Lord to reorder and change your life to
what is designed for a male or female. Ask Him to heal your
mind, will, and emotions.]

*Dear Heavenly Father, I repent for rejecting the true
identity that You have given me. I repent for injuring
my body in trying to change my gender identity. I
repent of self-hatred, and self-rejection, and taking
on the identity of a gender other than what I was created to be. I renounce all [female or male] unclean
or perverse spirits. I break every ungodly soul tie
with those I have had sex with. I renounce any false
marriage or partnership. I command unclean, perverse, impersonating spirits to leave me, as well as
all spirits of trauma and fear, in Jesus's name.*

I forgive those who caused me to hate myself, bought, misled, prostituted, or harmed me so that I performed these acts on my body.

I repent for degrading and rejecting my identity, and seeking to be a woman [if I am a man] or seeking to be a man [if I am a woman]. I forgive those who may have caused me to hate myself, and detach from my true identity, and I repent and forgive myself for self-hatred. I ask You, Lord, to fill in the gaps in my identity and the years that have been missing. Thank You for creating me a [man or woman].

Lord, take me back to my true identity and make me whole. Release me and cleanse me from the shame that pulls down my life and heart. Take away the barriers in my heart that have stopped me from realizing my true identity and loving myself. Heal my spirit, soul, and body. I know You love me and I receive Your love for me.

Repentance for Cross-dressers

I repent and renounce deliberately dressing like a member of the opposite sex, and I ask forgiveness for wanting to change my identity. Take away my attraction to clothes of the opposite sex, and help me to embrace who I am.

Repentance for Abortion

Dear Heavenly Father, I am sorry for aborting my child [or agreeing to the abortion of my child, or assisting with the abortion of a child]. I know this is the sin of murder, and I am sorry.

I release my child to You, knowing that we will be united one day.

I trust You to heal my life, and fill in the gap of emptiness. I repent for the generations before me, on my mother's side of the family, and my father's side of the family, for the sin of abortion, and I break every curse of abortion over my life. I command the spirits of trauma from abortion to leave me.

These prayers are just a starting point and there are many more steps in the delivering and healing process, but they open the door for the Lord to start bringing His life to your spirit, soul, and body. *Get help from your pastor, ministries targeted to your issues, Christian professionals, or mature believers.* Find a person you can be accountable to, and open your heart to the miracle working power of God.

Other actions you can take: Destroy all sexual literature in your home. Do not access sexually related websites on the Internet. Get rid of sexually explicit magazines, movies, and objects. Throw them away. These attract oppressive and unclean spirits, and bring heaviness and lust into your own house. Throw away sexual articles, and consider getting rid of gifts, clothes, and objects from former sexual partners. Anoint your house with oil and command anything unclean to leave. Ask the Lord to fill your heart and place.

Jesus said:

> If ye continue in my word, then ye are my disciples indeed; And ye shall know the truth, and the truth shall make you free.
>
> —JOHN 8:31–32

But if we walk in the light, as He is in the light, we have fellowship with one another, and the blood of Jesus Christ His Son cleanses us from all sin.

> —1 JOHN 1:7, NKJV

> If we confess our sins, He is faithful and just to forgive
> us our sins and to cleanse us from all unrighteousness.
>
> —1 John 1:9

The Lord wants to deal with us in many levels of transformation. Here are seven I recommend:

- Level one: Deals with the sin issue, repentance, and forgiveness. Without dealing with repentance and forgiveness, believers cannot move on to other areas of liberation.

- Level two: Demonic influence. Demonic spirits will leave or can be easily commanded to leave when we repent and agree with the truth of the Word of God.

- Level three: Generational curses, curses from disobedience, word curses from others (Jabez), and even ourselves, and occult curses.

- Level four: Breaking ungodly soul ties to people places and objects, even when these ties may exist in godly covenantal relationships. Soul ties can also occur with abuse and pornography. This also includes renouncing and breaking ungodly covenants and agreements with others.

- Level five: The meditations of our hearts, negative core beliefs, vows, renewing of the mind, dealing with grief, rejection, abandonment, shame, false selves, and defense mechanisms.

- Level six: Dying to self.

- Level seven: Dealing with deprivation, loss and legitimate needs that were never met, and areas of our personality that need growth, so that

the years that the locust and cankerworm have
eaten away can be filled in by the Lord.

Of course, ministry in these areas can be simultaneous, multilayered, and ongoing.

NOTES

PART I NOTES

1. Edythe Draper, *Draper's Book of Quotations for the Christian World* (Carol Stream, IL: Tyndale House Publishers, 1992).

2. Single Parent Success Foundation statistics at www.singleparentsuccess.org.

PART II NOTES

1. Strong's Greek Lexicon, s.v. *kardia*.

PART III NOTES

1. Joseph Nicolosi, *Shame and Attachment Loss: The Practical Work of Reparative Therapy* (Downers Grove, IL: InterVarsity Press, 2009), 37.

2. Elizabeth Moberly, *Homosexuality: A New Christian Ethic* (Cambridge: James Clarke & Co. Ltd, 1983).

PART IV NOTES

1. Jack W. Hayford, *Sex and the Single Soul* (Ventura, CA: Regal Books, 2005), 104.

2. Ibid, 106.

PART V NOTES

1. Mother Teresa's National Prayer Breakfast Speech Against Abortion (1994) can be found at http://www.orthodoxytoday.org/articles4/MotherTeresaAbortion.php (accessed March 30, 2012).

2. Ibid.

3. Ibid.

4. Dr. Angela Elizabeth Lanfranchi, M.D., FACS, "Abortion and Breast Cancer Links," March 2012.

ABOUT THE AUTHOR

Nancy Eskijian is Senior Pastor of Bread of Life Foursquare Gospel Church in Los Angeles, California, where she has served for more than seventeen years. Bread of Life is an urban church with English and Spanish spoken at every service, as well as a fusion of Jew and Gentile spiritual roots, ministering to needs of people, both spiritually and physically. She is also the author of *Restoration NOW!* a detailed resource on the ministry of inner healing and deliverance for ministers and laypersons to enable believers to reclaim their intended identity, inheritance and purpose in Christ.

CONTACT THE AUTHOR

WEBSITE:
WWW.LABREADOFLIFE.ORG

E-MAIL:
BREADOFLIFELA@GMAIL.COM

Made in the USA
Monee, IL
07 July 2026

56552447R10080